Artists

VOLUME 2: L-Z

FROM MICHELANGELO TO MAYA LIN

Artists

G. Aimée Ergas

U·X·L

AN IMPRINT OF GALE RESEARCH,
AN INTERNATIONAL THOMPSON PUBLISHING COMPANY

I(T)P

NEW YORK • LONDON • BONN • BOSTON • DETROIT • MADRID
MELBOURNE • MEXICO CITY • PARIS • SINGAPORE • TOKYO
TORONTO • WASHINGTON • ALBANY NY • BELMONT CA • CINCINNATI OH

10010224

Artists

From Michelangelo to Maya Lin

By G. Aimée Ergas

Staff

Carol DeKane Nagel, U·X·L Developmental Editor
Thomas L. Romig, U·X·L Publisher

Shanna P. Heilveil, Production Associate
Evi Seoud, Assistant Production Manager
Mary Beth Trimper, Production Director

Margaret A. Chamberlain, Permissions Associate (Pictures)

Pamela A. E. Galbreath, Art Director
Cynthia Baldwin, Product Design Manager

Cover Artwork: Leonardo da Vinci's *La Gioconda* (*Mona Lisa*; front left) reproduced by permission of Alinari/Art Resource; Andy Warhol portrait (front right) and Henry Moore's *King and Queen* (back left) reproduced by permission of Archive Photos/Express Newspapers.

Library of Congress Cataloging-in-Publication Data

Artists : from Michelangelo to Maya Lin
/ by G. Aimée Ergas.

xxxvi, 491 p. : ill. ; 25 cm.

Includes index.
Contents: v. 1. A-K — v. 2. L-Z
ISBN 0-8103-9862-1 (set); 0-8103-9863-X (v. 1); 0-8103-9864-8 (v. 2)
1. Artists—Biography—Juvenile literature. 2. Artists.
 I. Ergas, G. Aimée.

N42.E74 1995
7.09.22B—dc20   95-166826
                                                   CIP

Printed in the United States of America

10 9 8 7 6 5 4 3

To my loving husband and children,
who were very patient
with not being the center of my attention
during the creation of this work.

Contents

Salvador Dali

VOLUME 2: L-Z

Artists by Fields and Media

Bold numerals indicate volume numbers.

Alexander Calder

Architecture

Book and Magazine Illustration

Engraving

Environmental Art

Etching

Lithography

Masks

Mobiles

Mosaic

Mural

Needlework

Painting

Paper cutouts

Photography

Silk Screen

Stained Glass

Reader's Guide

Frida Kahlo

Artists: *From Michelangelo to Maya Lin* presents the life stories of 62 sculptors, painters, architects, photographers, illustrators, and designers whose works and ideas have changed the face of art. Concentrating on North American and European artists from the Renaissance to the modern day, *Artists* provides a view of the artists' worlds—their personal experiences and motivations and the social and artistic climates that informed their works—and the impact of their art on society and on future generations of artists.

Format

The 62 biographies of Artists are arranged alphabetically over two volumes. Each five- to ten-page entry opens with a portrait of the artist, birth and death information, and a quote by or about the artist. Accompanying several biographies are boxed sidebar pieces discussing important movements, events, or processes, such as impressionism, the famous Armory Show of 1913, and how sculpture is made. In addition to the 62 artists' portraits, nearly 140 works illustrate the text.

Each volume begins with a listing of the artists featured in the set by the fields in which they worked and their favored media, a time line showing a work by each artist alongside major historical events, and a glossary of key art terms, which appear in the text in boldface the first time they are used in an entry. The volumes conclude with a list of works for further reading and a cumulative subject index providing easy access to the people, movements, and works mentioned throughout *Artists*.

Comments and Suggestions

We welcome your comments on this work as well as your suggestions for individuals to be featured in future editions of *Artists: From Michelangelo to Maya Lin*. Please write: Author, *Artists*, U•X•L, 835 Penobscot Bldg., Detroit, Michigan 48226-4094; call toll-free: 1-800-877-4253; or fax 1-313-877-4253.

Words to Know

Henry O. Tanner

Abstract art: An art style in which the subject is not represented in a naturally recognizable manner. Instead of presenting the real appearance of the subject, abstract artists try to express ideas or feelings about the subject through the use of shapes, colors, lines, and other elements. **Wassily Kandinsky** (see entry) is credited with creating the first totally abstract painting. Although abstract art is primarily a modern style, there are elements of abstraction in ancient art, especially in the use of decorative patterns.

Abstract Expressionism: A movement of **abstract art** that emerged in New York City during the 1940s and reached its peak in the 1950s. Although abstract expressionists painted in many different styles, they had in common an interest in using paint to show their emotions. They often used thick and sometimes violent brush strokes to create dense textures on large canvases. These artists considered the actions involved in the creation of a painting—including the mistakes made in the process—to be as important as the finished work. Some important artists in this highly influential movement were **Jackson Pollock** (see entry), Mark Rothko, and Hans Hoffman.

Academic art: A term used to describe art that obeyed rules set down by the important art academy or school of the day. For example, in nineteenth-century Paris the most successful artists were those who painted in the style approved by the French Academy of Fine Arts, whose standards of beauty derived from ancient Greek and Roman culture. More adventurous artists used this term in a negative manner to describe art they felt was dull and uninventive. See also **Salon.**

Avante-garde: From a French word meaning "vanguard" or "ahead of its time." When applied to art, avant-garde describes creations that are progressive, innovative, or experimental. Since it challenges established styles, avant-garde work is often controversial.

Baroque: An art style developed in the early 1600s and lasting into the early 1700s. The main characteristic of this style is its sense of unity among the arts of painting, architecture, and sculpture. Reacting against the classical and sometimes severe style of **Renaissance** art, baroque artists sought to make their works more lively and emotional. With an emphasis on bright colors, light, and exaggerated forms, many Baroque compositions exhibit a feeling of energy and movement. Baroque style later developed into **rococo** art. Notable baroque artists include **Rembrandt van Rijn, Peter Paul Rubens,** and **Diego Velazquez** (see entries).

Collage: From a French word meaning "gluing" or "pasting." A collage is an artistic composition created when such unrelated materials as cloth, newspaper, wallpaper, string, and wire are combined and pasted on a painted or unpainted surface. **Pablo Picasso** (see entry) was one of the first modern artists to use this technique. See also **photocollage.**

Color field painting: A painting style that emphasizes color as its only element. Most color field works are created on large canvases. Combining skilled technique with a sharp sense of color, artists in this style produce works that give the illusion of depth and light. From the mid-1950s to the mid-1960s, **Helen Frankenthaler** (see entry), Morris Louis, and Kenneth Noland were prominent color field artists.

Cubism: An art movement begun in the early 1900s by **Pablo Picasso** (see entry) and Georges Braque. Cubist artists abandoned the desire to render a subject with mood and emotion. Instead, they presented it broken apart into geometric shapes. In this way, they depicted the subject from several points of view at once—an attempt to portray the subject not as the eye sees it but as the mind perceives it. Cubism was one of the most important developments in modern art.

Dadaism: A literary and art movement that began in Switzerland in 1916 and lasted until 1922. Disillusioned by the effects of World War I, dada artists fought against traditional artistic values, creating art that showed absurd, nonsensical, and violent aspects of life. Some prominent dada artists were **Marcel Duchamp, Man Ray** (see entries), and Hans Arp.

Engraving: A method of printmaking whereby lines and grooves are cut with a sharp tool into a metal plate (or in some instance a wood block) and then filled with ink. After the surface of the plate is wiped clean, the plate is pressed against absorbent paper, producing an image from the pooled ink. Engravings can be original works by an artist or a way of copying an existing work. See also **etching** and **woodcut.**

Environmental art: Art that makes use of elements of natural or urban surroundings, including light, landscape, architecture, and sound, as part of the artistic creation. These works often take up large areas of space, such as city plazas or open fields. Forces of nature—like rain and sunlight—also play an important role in the effect and interpretation of the composition. Most environmental art works are temporary; photography and video are used to document the works. **Christo** (see entry) is the best-known environmental artist of our time.

Etching: A method of **engraving** that uses a metal plate covered with a layer of acid-resistant wax. The artist draws through the wax with a sharp instrument to reveal portions of the metal plate. Next the plate is dipped in acid, which attacks only the parts where the wax has been scraped away. The plate is covered with ink, then the surface is wiped clean. Afterward, paper is pressed onto the inked plate. The etched portion of the plate, which retains the ink, reveals the artist's drawing. An etching may be printed several times.

Expressionism: A term used to describe art in which the personal feeling of the artist is the most important aspect of the work. Instead of imitating real life, expressionist artists transform it to fit their creative visions. Colors, shapes, and textures are often exaggerated to show emotion. The art of **Vincent van Gogh** (see entry) is a well-known example of expressionism. Expressionist styles often have a descriptive word to identify them more specifically, such as **abstract expressionism** or German expressionism.

Fauvism: A brief art movement begun by **Henri Matisse** (see entry) and other artists in the early twentieth century. They were interested in using only pure, strong colors to define structure, to generate light, and to capture emotion in their paintings. Because the use of color in the resulting works seemed violent and uncontrolled, critics called these artists "fauves," which means "wild beasts" in French.

Folk art: The traditional art of the native inhabitants of a region whose artists have not received any formal artistic training. Many professional artists have used ideas from folk art in their works.

Fresco: From the Italian word for "fresh." A fresco is a wall painting made with pigments, the powdery substances used to make paint. The pigments are mixed with water and applied quickly to a plastered wall while the plaster is still wet. As the plaster dries, the pigment colors are absorbed into the plaster, retaining their bright hues. This technique was perfected during the Italian **Renaissance**, especially by **Michelangelo**. Fresco painting declined until the modern era, when **Diego Rivera** (see entries) sparked a renewed interest in the technique.

Impressionism: The most important movement in European art in the late 1800s. Impressionist artists, who were mostly French, explored new theories about light and color. Rather than copying a scene exactly as it looked, they used these theories to capture the "impression" of a scene as they viewed it. They were interested in the ways atmosphere and light changed the way things appeared in nature. Many styles of modern art developed from the ideas of the impressionists. Some important impressionist painters were **Claude Monet, Pierre-Auguste Renoir, Edouard Manet** (see entries), and Edgar Degas.

Kinetic art: A term describing sculpture that includes motion as a distinctive element of the work. The kinetic sculptures of **Alexander Calder** (see entry), called mobiles, are among the earliest kinetic art works.

Lithograph: A print made by drawing with a special grease crayon on a porous stone or on a grained metal plate. When water is applied to the stone or plate and ink is rolled across it, the water does not stick to the crayoned areas, but the ink does. Paper is then pressed onto the stone or plate and the retained ink prints the drawing. A lithograph can be printed several times.

Mosaic: A design made by setting small pieces of colored glass, stone, tile, wood, or other material in cement. Mosaics are often used to decorate floors or walls.

Mural: A large painting on a wall or attached to a wall. A **fresco** is one type of mural.

Op art: Short for optical art, this style became popular in the 1960s when op artists began using bright colors and intricate patterns to create illusions of movement and other effects to fool a viewer's eyes.

Perspective: A method used by artists to create the illusion of depth on a flat surface or in relief sculpture. Artists use perspective to show an object in the distance or to show the relation among objects of various sizes. Perspective was an important element of **Renaissance** art; **Leonardo da Vinci** (see entry) studied and perfected the rules of perspective drawing.

Photocollage: Also known as photomontage, a photocollage is made by combining parts of unrelated photographs into a singular composition.

Pointillism: A method of painting whereby an artist places separate, small dots of pure color side by side on a canvas. The result is such that the viewer's eyes naturally combine the colors to produce the illusion of brighter or more varied colors than if the paints had been mixed. This method was developed by late-nineteenth-century French painter **Georges Seurat** (see entry).

Pop art: An art style that emerged in England in the late 1950s as a reaction against the seriousness of **abstract expressionism** and peaked in the 1960s with the works of **Andy Warhol** and **Roy Lichtenstein** (see entries). In an attempt to marry popular culture and high art, pop artists used such images as cartoons, advertisements, movie stars, rock singers, and consumer items in their often humorous works.

Realism: A mid-nineteenth-century art style whose followers attempted to depict objects and scenes as they existed in real life, without any attempt to make them perfect or ideal. Realist artists focused on scenes of everyday life (most often the "ugly" or commonplace) rather than on biblical or heroic subjects or characters. See also **social realism**.

Renaissance: From a French word meaning "rebirth." The Renaissance was a period of heightened artistic and intellectual activity prompted by a renewed interest in the art and literature of the ancient Greeks and Romans. It began in Italy in the late 1300s and spread through Europe by the 1600s. During the Renaissance, great advances were made in areas such as science and exploration, music, literature, and the visual arts. **Michelangelo** and **Leonardo da Vinci** (see entries) were two significant Renaissance artists.

Rococo: A decorative style of art and architecture that began in eighteenth-century France and rapidly spread across Europe. A reaction to the heaviness of **baroque** decoration, the rococo is marked by delicacy and light and common motifs include shells, scrolls, leaves, and other curving shapes.

Salon: An annual exhibition of art works selected by jury and sponsored by the French Academy of Fine Arts beginning in 1737. Until the mid-nineteenth century, when the juries began to favor conservative, established art styles, it was considered a great honor for an artist's work to be exhibited in one of these influential shows. See also **academic art**.

Social realism: A form of **realism** embraced by American artists of the 1920s and 1930s who wanted to use their art to make political and economic statements about society. These artists usually depicted the lives of workers, the poor, and the homeless. Social realism is not defined by one particular artistic style but by subject content. For instance, both **Jacob Lawrence** and **Diego Rivera** (see entries) are social realists.

Still life: A work of art whose subject is inanimate objects such as flowers, fruits and vegetables, pottery, tableware, and other decorative pieces.

Surrealism: A literary and art movement founded by writer André Breton in Paris in 1924 and practiced internationally into the 1930s. It was grounded in the psychoanalytic theories of Sigmund Freud, particularly those relating to the expression of the imagination as revealed in dreams. Using a range of styles, the surrealists, such as **Salvador Dali** (see entry) and René Magritte, filled their works with fantastic imagery and dream-inspired symbols.

Woodcut: Also known as a woodblock print, a woodcut is a print made from designs cut in relief on wood. The area that is not to be printed as part of the design is carved away. Ink is then rolled on the remaining surface area and paper is applied to the block to produce the desired print. **Albrecht Dürer** (see entry) was a master of the woodblock print, the oldest method of printmaking. The designs of Japanese woodblock prints exhibited in Paris in the late nineteenth century inspired many of the impressionist painters.

Events in Art and History

1501-04 Michelangelo, *David*

1503-05 Leonardo da Vinci, *La Gioconda* (*Mona Lisa*)

1513 Albrecht Dürer, *Knight, Death, and Devil*

1545 Titian, *Portrait of Pope Paul III with His Grandsons*

1565 Pieter Bruegel, *The Peasant Wedding*

1600 El Greco, *View of Toledo*

1623 Peter Paul Rubens, *Maria de Medici, Queen of France, Landing in Marseilles*

Vietnam Veterans Memorial by Maya Lin

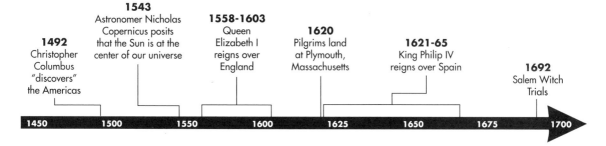

1492
Christopher Columbus "discovers" the Americas

1543
Astronomer Nicholas Copernicus posits that the Sun is at the center of our universe

1558-1603
Queen Elizabeth I reigns over England

1620
Pilgrims land at Plymouth, Massachusetts

1621-65
King Philip IV reigns over Spain

1692
Salem Witch Trials

1450   1500   1550   1600   1625   1650   1675   1700

1642 Rembrandt van Rijn, *The Night Watch*

1656 Diego Velazquez, *Las Meninas* (*Maids of Honor*)

1814 Francisco Goya, *Tres de Mayo, 1808*
(*The Third of May, 1808*)

1842 J. M. W. Turner, *Snowstorm: Steamer off a
Harbour's Mouth*

1863 Edouard Manet, *Le Déjeuner sur l'herbe*
(*Luncheon on the Grass*)

1872 Claude Monet, *Impression: Sunrise*

1876 Pierre-Auguste Renoir, *Le Moulin de la Galette*

1880 Auguste Rodin, *The Thinker*

1884-1926 Antonio Gaudi, Church of the Sagrada Familia,
Barcelona, Spain

1885 Georges Seurat, *A Sunday Afternoon on
the Island of La Grand Jatte*

1886 Mary Cassatt, *Girl Arranging Her Hair*

1889 Vincent van Gogh, *The Starry Night*

1893 Henry O. Tanner, *The Banjo Lesson*

1893-95 Henri de Toulouse-Lautrec, *At the Moulin Rouge*

1897 Paul Gauguin, *Where Do We Come From?
What Are We? Where Are We Going?*

1898 Paul Cézanne, *Mont Sainte-Victoire
from Bibemus Quarry*

1907 Pablo Picasso, *Les Demoiselles d'Avignon*

1907 Alfred Stieglitz, *The Steerage*

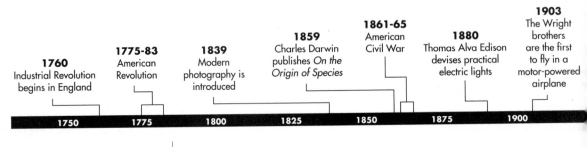

1760
Industrial Revolution
begins in England

1775-83
American
Revolution

1839
Modern
photography is
introduced

1859
Charles Darwin
publishes *On the
Origin of Species*

1861-65
American
Civil War

1880
Thomas Alva Edison
devises practical
electric lights

1903
The Wright
brothers
are the first
to fly in a
motor-powered
airplane

| 1750 | 1775 | 1800 | 1825 | 1850 | 1875 | 1900 |

1908   Henri Matisse, *Harmony in Red*

1911   Marc Chagall, *I and the Village*

1912   Marcel Duchamp, *Nude Descending a Staircase, No. 2*

1913   Wassily Kandinsky, *Improvisation 30 (Cannons)*

1921   Stuart Davis, *Lucky Strike*

1923   Man Ray, *Violon d'Ingres*

1925   Kathe Kollwitz, *Bread!*

1925-26   Walter Gropius, Bauhaus, Dessau, Germany

1927   Ansel Adams, *Monolith—The Face of Half Dome, Yosemite National Park, California, 1927*

1928   Constantin Brancusi, *Bird in Space*

1928-29   Diego Rivera, *The Struggle of the Classes*

1929   Augusta Savage, *Gamin*

1931   Salvador Dali, *Persistence de la mémoire (The Persistence of Memory)*

1931   Georgia O'Keeffe, *Cow's Skull: Red, White, and Blue*

1932   Berenice Abbott, *Nightview, New York, 1932*

1934   Alexander Calder, *Calderberry Bush*

1936   Frida Kahlo, *My Grandparents, My Parents and I*

1936-39   Frank Lloyd Wright, Fallingwater, the Kaufmann House, Bear Run, Pennsylvania

1938   Henri Cartier-Bresson, *Banks of the Marne*

1941   Jacob Lawrence, *And the Migrants Kept Coming*

1942   Edward Hopper, *Nighthawks*

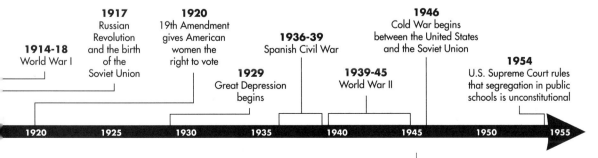

1914-18
World War I

1917
Russian Revolution and the birth of the Soviet Union

1920
19th Amendment gives American women the right to vote

1929
Great Depression begins

1936-39
Spanish Civil War

1939-45
World War II

1946
Cold War begins between the United States and the Soviet Union

1954
U.S. Supreme Court rules that segregation in public schools is unconstitutional

1920   1925   1930   1935   1940   1945   1950   1955

Events in Art and History

1942 Piet Mondrian, *Broadway Boogie-Woogie*

1950 Jackson Pollock, *Lavender Mist: Number 1, 1950*

1951-52 Isamu Noguchi, *Mu*

1952 Helen Frankenthaler, *Mountains and Sea*

1957-58 Henry Moore, *UNESCO Reclining Figure*

1961 Andy Warhol, *32 Soup Cans*

1962 Roy Lichtenstein, *Blam!*

1964 Romare Bearden, *Projections*

1967 David Hockney, *A Bigger Splash*

1970 Duane Hanson, *Tourists*

1979 Judy Chicago, *The Dinner Party*

1980 Maya Lin, *Vietnam Veterans Memorial*

1986 Faith Ringgold, *Harlem Renaissance Party*

1989-93 I. M. Pei, Le Grande Louvre, Paris, France

1992 Annie Leibovitz, *Demi Moore*

1995 Christo, *Wrapped Reichstag, Project for Berlin*

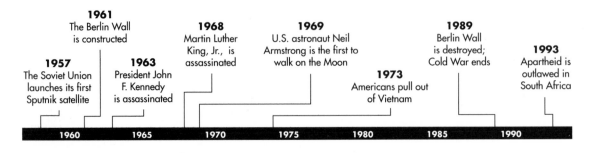

1961
The Berlin Wall
is constructed

1957
The Soviet Union
launches its first
Sputnik satellite

1963
President John
F. Kennedy
is assassinated

1968
Martin Luther
King, Jr., is
assassinated

1969
U.S. astronaut Neil
Armstrong is the first to
walk on the Moon

1973
Americans pull out
of Vietnam

1989
Berlin Wall
is destroyed;
Cold War ends

1993
Apartheid is
outlawed in
South Africa

1960   1965   1970   1975   1980   1985   1990

Artists

Jacob Lawrence

Born September 7, 1917
Atlantic City, New Jersey

Jacob Lawrence was one of the first African American artists to rise to prominence in the mainstream American art world. He was encouraged by teachers and fellow artists during his teenage years to study both art and African American history. He combined these interests to produce works unique in both their subject and style. Many of these comprise series of panels that join together to create a narrative. Lawrence is also known as an illustrator of books for adults and children.

In the early part of the twentieth century, huge numbers of African Americans migrated from the rural South to the cities of the North. They hoped to find jobs in growing industries, particularly on the automobile assembly lines of Detroit, Michigan. Lawrence's parents, Jacob Armstead Lawrence and Rose Lee, were among these migrants. They met and married in Atlantic City, New Jersey. The oldest of their three children, Jacob, was born there in 1917. During Lawrence's childhood, his family was forced to relocate many times as his parents looked for

"I paint the things I know about, the things I have experienced. The things I have experienced extend into my national, racial, and class group. So I paint the American scene."

▲ *Portrait: Reproduced by permission of AP/Wide World Photos.*

Jacob Lawrence

work. Steady jobs were hard to find, especially for African Americans. Racial prejudice prevented them from pursuing certain jobs or professions. These many moves had a disruptive effect on Lawrence, who was a quiet and sensitive boy; he found it difficult to constantly adjust to new neighborhoods and schools.

Moved to Harlem during Renaissance

The hardest adjustment of all came when he was 13. It was then that he went to live with his mother in Harlem, the mostly African American section of New York City. It was a crowded, teeming place, and the public school Lawrence attended was considered among the roughest in the area. But Harlem in the 1930s was also the center of what became known as the Harlem Renaissance. Many African American artists, writers, musicians, and scholars lived there. It was a time of great creativity and excitement.

To keep her son out of trouble, Rose Lawrence enrolled him in an after-school arts and crafts program at a local community center. It was taught by a young African American artist named Charles Alston. Alston liked the serious, quiet Lawrence and made sure he had lots of materials for his efforts: soap to carve, reeds to make baskets, crayons and pencils for drawing, wood for construction. "I decided then that I wanted to be an artist," Lawrence later wrote. He found that drawing geometric designs in bright colors satisfied him greatly. He soon moved on to elaborate patterns and developed his own method of painting in which particular shapes were rendered in corresponding colors, one at a time; he would paint all the triangles in red, then do all the squares in yellow, and so on. Lawrence continued in this mode through much of his career. This notable consistency of color is apparent in the artist's later series of story panels.

Alston recognized that the young Lawrence was a significant talent. He remarked in later years that Lawrence never asked like the other children, "What should I do next?" He always had a project in mind and simply needed information to help him complete it. Alston told many of his artist friends about this gifted young man. They frequently visited the class to see his work and encourage him. Lawrence quickly became known among the artistic circles of Harlem.

Lawrence got many of his ideas from the books and magazines he found at the center where the classes were held. He once came across an article about a famous artist who made papier-maché masks. Lawrence had Alston show him how to mix papier-maché, and he went on to create many colorful, life-size masks. He also used cardboard boxes to fashion three-sided scenes depicting locales in Harlem—stores, barbershops, houses, and newsstands. These were like miniature theater sets, though Lawrence had never been to the theater.

During the time he worked with Alston, Lawrence found little at school to interest him. After two years of high school he dropped out, despite his mother's protests. This was during the Great Depression, and jobs were extremely scarce. Lawrence was able to earn only meager funds by selling old bottles and running errands. He continued to paint whenever he could, but times were hard. Then, in 1936, Lawrence was accepted into the Civilian Conservation Corps (CCC), a government program designed to get young men out of the cities to work on projects such as planting trees and building roads and dams. Lawrence's CCC service taught him many new skills and made him think that perhaps painting should be only a hobby.

Enters Depression-era funding program

He returned to New York but still could find no work besides odd jobs. He again began attending art classes at various community centers, including one offered by the acclaimed sculptor **Augusta Savage** (see entry). Like Alston, Savage recognized Lawrence's talent and took him under her wing. She soon realized that Lawrence was having difficulty earning money. She took him to a government office to enroll him in a project that helped support artists. But Lawrence was not eligible because he was only 20 years old and not the required 21. Lawrence was extremely disappointed and continued looking for other work. Savage did not give up, however. She waited a year and on Lawrence's twenty-first birthday, she took him back to the government office to sign him up. He was accepted and offered $25 a week, a comfortable living in those days. He was free to do what he wanted as long as he produced two paintings every six weeks. Lawrence later stated, "If Augusta Savage hadn't insisted on getting me on the project, I would never have become an artist. It was a real turning point for me."

For about a year and a half, Lawrence was able to take classes, hone his painting skills, and put concerns about money out of his mind. Through the funding project he met many other artists and writers. They gathered in each other's studios to exchange ideas about art, literature, and life in general. Lawrence's paintings from this period are mostly scenes of Harlem, among them *Clinic* and *Bar 'N Grill.* He was able to keenly illustrate how hard it was to survive during the Depression years. Through color, pattern, and exaggerated form, he expressed weariness and despair.

During these years Lawrence regularly attended a discussion group focusing on African and African American history held at the local public library. It was led by a prominent scholar, Charles Seifert. Seifert applauded Lawrence's interest and encouraged him to study American history in depth, especially the role of African Americans. The artist had never learned this history in school. Now he uncovered many critical events and heroes forgotten by the public school system. These discoveries provided him with subjects for many of his works.

Lawrence was particularly drawn to the life story of Francis Dominique Toussaint, known as Toussaint L'Ouverture, the military leader of eighteenth-century Haiti, who overthrew the slave system and liberated the Caribbean island nation from French domination. Lawrence read everything he could about Toussaint and decided to paint a record of his achievements. But one painting was not enough. Lawrence ultimately unveiled a series of 41 panels, beginning with Christopher Columbus's "discovery" of Haiti and then outlining Toussaint's childhood, battles, and death in a French prison. The settings of the scenes employed a great measure of realism, but Lawrence used intense color and exaggeration to express the emotional power of this hero.

This series and later ones have been compared to movie stills or slides that narrate a story as the viewer progresses through them. Lawrence continued in this method, portraying the lives of several African American heroes, including Harriet Tubman, a leader of the Underground Railroad of antislavery forces who smuggled slaves North; writer and abolitionist Frederick Douglass; and John Brown, a white abolitionist who led a slave revolt in Virginia. In all of these works, he used his formidable artistic skills to conjure the struggle for freedom and justice, forcefully representing the strength of character of his subjects.

Exhibited L'Ouverture series at 22

Lawrence was only 22 when he completed the Toussaint L'Ouverture series in 1938. It received much attention for its unusual subject matter and praise for its artistry. Two acquaintances of Lawrence prominent in the art world arranged for the panels to be included in an exhibition at the Baltimore Museum of Art. This was the first major museum to feature an exhibition by African American artists. An entire room was devoted to Lawrence's panels. The exhibition won him great recognition and several fellowships.

Lawrence was encouraged by his success to begin work on still another series. This one told the story of the many African Americans who migrated to the cities of the North around World War I. The 60 panels were created from accounts he gathered from family members, his own childhood experiences, and exhaustive research. Painted in Lawrence's bold, geometric style, with many vivid colors, they depict the hard life of the migrants, but also their courage and dignity. In 1992 Lawrence published a book, *The Great Migration,* using many panels from the series. In the introduction he wrote, "Uprooting yourself from one way of life to make your way in another involves conflict and struggle. But out of the struggle comes a kind of power, and even beauty. I tried to convey this in the rhythm of the pictures, and in the repetition of certain images." The Migration series was another triumph.

About this time Lawrence married a young painter he had met through Savage named Gwendolyn Knight. She became indispensable to his career, frequently helping him prepare his panels. But more important, Knight offered unflagging support when Lawrence encountered various artistic and emotional obstacles in later years.

Lawrence served in the Coast Guard during World War II, from 1943 to 1945. He was a steward's mate, the only rating available to African Americans because the military was segregated by race in those days. Lawrence was lucky to be selected for the Coast Guard's first racially integrated crew. The crew commander knew of his artistic career and secured Lawrence a position as a public relations officer. He was assigned to paint a record of life in the Coast Guard. The troopship he served on sailed to Italy, Egypt, and India. Lawrence's Coast Guard paintings were shown at several museums after the war.

Doubts of "America's number one black painter"

Lawrence's reputation grew quickly in the postwar years. He was called "America's number one black painter." But this phrase troubled him because it seemed to suggest two different criteria of value, one for black artists and a different one for "real" artists. During this time Lawrence also found it difficult locating new subjects for his paintings. Trends in art were changing, too. **Abstract art,** that which focused on the emotional rather than the physical realm, was beginning to dominate the art world.

These forces combined to create doubt in Lawrence's mind about his talents and abilities; he began to question his success and wonder if it were not just luck that got him where he was. His anxiety became so severe that in 1949 he entered a hospital to seek treatment. Lawrence felt that his two years there greatly helped him reconcile his feelings and increase his understanding of his place in the world. His work of the 1950s reflects this new peace. Perhaps the most important series from these years is *Struggle: From the History of the American People.* These 30 paintings display key events in U.S. history, emphasizing the role of ordinary people of all races and heritages.

Despite Lawrence's doubts, the art world continued to honor him. In 1953 he was the first African American artist to receive a large grant from the National Institute of Arts and Letters and the first elected a member of the Institute in 1965. In 1983 he was only the second African American elected to the 50-member American Academy of Arts and Letters. He also received the National Medal of Arts from President George Bush in 1990. These are just a few of the many awards Lawrence has received.

Masterworks

1938	*Toussaint L'Ouverture*
1939	*Harriet Tubman*
1941	*And the Migrants Kept Coming*
1942	*John Brown*
1946	*War*
1956	*Struggle: From the History of the American People*

Jacob Lawrence

*Christmas Pageant, 1952.
Reproduced by permission
of The Bettmann Archive.*

Since the 1960s Lawrence has spent much of his time teaching. He was a professor of art at the University of Washington in Seattle for many years. Most recently he has dedicated his talents to book illustration. His panels from the Harriet Tubman series were published in a volume called *Harriet and the Promised Land* in 1967. And in 1970 he lent his hand to an edition of Aesop's Fables. In addition to the publication of his book *The Great Migration,* the early 1990s saw his panels about abolitionist John Brown published in *John Brown: One Man against Slavery.* In all of these endeavors, Lawrence has labored to reveal the commitment to freedom and justice of people struggling for life's most basic needs and in so doing, miraculously maintaining their humanity and a sense of hope.

Annie Leibovitz

Born October 2, 1949
Westbury, Connecticut

She is "a photographer of celebrities who has herself be come a celebrity." For the past 25 years, no photographer has delivered more photographs of the people we most want to see than has Annie Leibovitz. Her pictures are recognizable for their bright colors, intense lighting, and above all, for unique and surprising poses. In magazine spreads and advertising campaigns, Leibovitz has demonstrated that she is a master of projecting the popular culture of our time.

Anna-Lou Leibovitz was born in Westbury, Connecticut. Her father, Sam Leibovitz, was an Air Force lieutenant colonel and because of his career, the family moved often during Leibovitz's childhood. Her mother, Marilyn Leibovitz, was a modern-dance instructor and the chief force in raising Annie and her five siblings. Leibovitz remembers taking many dance classes from her mother and other teachers. She credits this for her later interest in photographing dancers.

"When you trust your point of view, that's when you start taking pictures."

▲ *Portrait: Reproduced by permission of AP/Wide World Photos.*

| Annie Leibovitz

During high school Leibovitz played guitar and wrote music and was the head of the school folksinging club. She also developed an interest in painting and attended the San Francisco Art Institute, beginning in 1967. She considered a career as a painting instructor. During a vacation from school, Leibovitz visited her family, then living in the Philippines. She and her mother took a trip to Japan, where she bought a camera and began taking pictures.

When she returned to school, Leibovitz enrolled in a night class in photography. "I was totally seduced by the wonderment of it all," she told a writer for *ArtNews*. "To see something that afternoon and have it materialize before your eyes that same day. There was a real immediacy to it. I lived in the darkroom."

Begins long association with *Rolling Stone*

From then on Leibovitz was hooked on photography. She worked on a kibbutz, a collectively run farm, in Israel for several months in 1969. She took pictures while there and continued to snap away when she returned to California. In 1970 a friend suggested that she take her prints to *Rolling Stone* magazine, which was headquartered in San Francisco. *Rolling Stone* was just getting started then, a new magazine about rock music and the counterculture that had emerged in the late 1960s from the bohemia of the 1950s. Jann Wenner, the magazine's founder, was impressed by Leibovitz's photos. He began giving her assignments, paying her $47 a week before she had even graduated from college. Leibovitz recalled, "I can never forget the sensation of being at a newsstand and seeing for the first time my photograph transformed into the *Rolling Stone* cover."

By 1973, when she was only 23 years old, Leibovitz had become chief photographer for *Rolling Stone;* she stayed with the magazine for ten more years. During that time she traveled around the country and the world photographing everyone who was anyone in pop music. Her reputation was cemented by photographs of two subjects. One was former

Beatle John Lennon. She snapped countless shots of Lennon between 1970 and his death in 1980. One of her most famous photographs was taken on December 8, 1980, only two hours before Lennon's murder.

The second subject that would spread Leibovitz's renown was the English group the Rolling Stones; she was hired by the band in 1975 to document their concert tour of that

Steve Martin in Tails, December 1981. Color photograph. Reproduced by permission of Annie Leibovitz/Contact Press Images.

year. The photographs she produced as she traveled and lived with the Stones have been called "some of the most eloquent images ever made of the world of Rock and Roll." That project and growing acclaim for *Rolling Stone* made Leibovitz a big name among contemporary photographers. Unfortunately, she became associated with drugs as well as with rock and roll; the pressure of her career and nearness to rock's excesses led her to begin using cocaine. "I went on that [Rolling Stones] tour to get to the heart of something, to see what it was like," she later told *Vanity Fair.* "People always talk about the soul of the sitter [in a photograph], but the photographer has a soul, too. And I almost lost it." Leibovitz has admitted that it took her five years to "get off the tour," but she did, and her career continued to climb.

Develops signature style with color

Leibovitz's early photographs were in black and white. When *Rolling Stone* began printing in color in 1974, she started using color film, staging elaborate scenes for the magazine's covers. She explained to *ArtNews,* "When I was in school, I wasn't taught anything about lighting, I was only taught black-and-white. So I had to learn about color myself." Nonetheless, Leibovitz quickly developed her signature style, notable for brilliant color, partly because it printed well.

During her years with *Rolling Stone* and in her work for other magazines, Leibovitz photographed many of the biggest names in entertainment, including keyboardist-singer Stevie Wonder, rocker Bruce Springsteen, film director Woody Allen, country songbird Dolly Parton, pop singer Linda Ronstadt, actress Meryl Streep, dancer Mikhail Baryshnikov, and action film star Arnold Schwarzenegger. Initially her photographs of celebrities were like snapshots, capturing the subject in the moment. But she soon became aware of her ability to put people at ease, helping them to "let down their guard." She encouraged her famous subjects to pose for her doing crazy or silly things that frequently revealed their personalities more than just a "straight" portrait could. Another secret of Leibovitz's success is her careful pre-shoot research of her subjects: she reads their books or poetry, sees their movies or performances, and when possible, spends time observing their daily lives.

Her best-known photographs feature actress Whoopi Goldberg with only her face, arms, and legs peeking out of a bathtub full of milk; TV star Roseanne mud-wrestling with her husband Tom Arnold; and the artist **Christo** (see entry) wrapped in fabric like one of his artworks. Photography writer and critic Andy Grundberg pointed out how Leibovitz "exaggerates the distinctive characteristic of [the celebrities'] public image in a way that's funny and deflating." Perhaps her most controversial photograph was for a 1992 *Vanity Fair* cover; on it appeared actress Demi Moore—nude and very pregnant.

Broadens reputation at *Vanity Fair*

In 1983 Leibovitz left *Rolling Stone;* shortly thereafter she became chief photographer for *Vanity Fair.* This afforded her the opportunity to photograph even more stars, including many artists, writers, poets, and dancers. That year she also mounted her first solo show, many of her portraits numbering among its 60 pictures. A reviewer for the *Christian Science Monitor* attested of Leibovitz's work: "There is humor and beauty here, as well as images that some may consider downright outrageous.... She goes a step beyond what is necessary to create striking images of famous people."

In 1986 Leibovitz added advertising to her list of assignments. She has contributed her photographs to the ad campaigns of numerous companies, among them Honda, Arrow shirts, Rose's Lime Juice, the Gap, and American Express. Her work on behalf of the latter earned her the coveted Clio Award, the equivalent of an Academy Award, from the ad-

Masterworks

1971	*Christmas, Soledad Prison, California*
1975	*Mick Jagger, Chicago*
1978	*Muhammad Ali, Chicago*
1980	*John Lennon and Yoko Ono, New York City*
1981	*Steve Martin in Tails*
1984	*Bruce Springsteen, New York City*
1985	*Sting, Lucerne Valley, California*
1989	*Magic Johnson*

vertising industry. Leibovitz says that some of the success of these photographs can be attributed to large budgets, most notably from American Express, which enabled her to fly her subjects to virtually any locale and allowed her to spend several days photographing them. "I've moved into the terrain of making pictures, composing, theatre," she told *New York* magazine.

In 1991 Leibovitz was honored with a major exhibition at the National Portrait Gallery in Washington, D.C. It was only the second display of the work of a living photographer ever mounted at the site. The exhibit drew more visitors during its five weeks than ordinarily visit the National Portrait Gallery in an entire year. A book was published to accompany the show titled *Photographs: Annie Leibovitz 1970-1990.* It contains almost 200 of her photos, dating back to her kibbutz days in 1969. In the early 1990s Leibovitz's work was shown in Arizona, Florida, Utah, Boston, and San Francisco, to name just a few of its destinations.

Leibovitz herself is quite recognizable—tall, with lanky blonde hair, a prominent nose, and a broad smile. Despite the exposure she has received over the years and the stars with whom she has hobnobbed, she claims to be quite shy. An exercise enthusiast, she maintains an apartment in New York City and a home on Long Island but spends much of her time traveling on assignment. The photographer has said she sometimes regrets not having much time for her personal life, conceding, "My longest relationship has always been my work. My work has always delivered for me." But she has also claimed, "I'm happy doing exactly what I'm doing.... I can do this the rest of my life. It's only going to get better."

Despite its popularity, Leibovitz's work has received some criticism that it is superficial because of its emphasis on celebrities. More often, however, critics comment on how much her celebrity photographs reveal about their subject and about contemporary American culture. Leibovitz has said that it is important to her to study the work of earlier artists and photographers. Yet the unusual poses, vivid lighting, and unexpected elements in her portraiture indicate a totally modern vision. The reflection of culture and society has been the goal of many artists; Annie Leibovitz has amply achieved this aim with her camera.

Leonardo da Vinci

Born April 15, 1452
Vinci, Italy
Died May 2, 1519
Cloux, France

"Among the studies of natural effects, light is the one that elates the most those who contemplate it."

▲ *Portrait:* Self-portrait. *Reproduced by permission of The Bettmann Archive.*

Leonardo Da Vinci might be called the original Renaissance Man, due not only to the period in which he lived but also to his brilliant versatility. The list of his skills and occupations is staggering: painter, writer, inventor, architect, botanist, engineer, mathematician, musician, city planner, philosopher, costume and set designer. He tackled each field of endeavor with great intensity, developing new and often startling ideas. Leonardo integrated the range of his expertise into every undertaking; his artwork inevitably showcased his scientific and philosophical background. During his life and consistently since his death, Leonardo has been revered by artists, scientists, scholars, popes, and kings.

Leonardo was raised in the mountain town of Vinci in central Italy. His parents were not married, and no clear records exist detailing his early days. It is known, however, that by the time he was five, he was living in his grandfather's house with his father, Ser Piero da Vinci, and stepmother. Leonardo's prodigious talent and intelligence manifested themselves quite early; he immersed himself in observing and drawing subjects from nature and drawing and making models of machines. He also loved horses and was an accomplished rider, and he maintained a sizable menagerie of animals, including bats, snakes, and newts. Apparently, Leonardo's essential problem was that he was interested in so many things that he would often excitedly take up projects—only to drop them unfinished when the next intriguing challenge came along.

The family eventually moved to Florence, then a center of great artistic and scholarly activity. When Leonardo was about 17, his father sent him to study in the workshop of a well-known painter, Andrea del Verrocchio. He spent several years there practicing painting and drawing, though few details are available about his life at this time. One story alleges that when Verrocchio finally let Leonardo paint one part of a commissioned painting, the artist was so astounded by the student's talent—especially Leonardo's use of color—that he never painted again. Surely the truth of this anecdote is questionable, but Leonardo's exceptional ability to employ color to illustrate the texture of skin, drapery, animal fur, and plant foliage was widely recognized.

Draws studies of anatomy and machinery

Leonardo drew constantly, filling notebooks with depictions of faces, plants, flowers, rocks, machines, and animals. He considered it the artist's duty to understand the structure of things he wanted to draw; this conviction led him to the study of anatomy, especially the workings of the muscles and the science of optics—how the eye sees. He was equally curious about the physical elements, conducting experiments on the properties of light, air, and weather. Museums retain pages and pages of his studies for all sorts of machines, bridges, carriages, tanks, and other military equipment—even flying machines. Perhaps to prevent the theft of his ideas, Leonardo penned notes for his studies and drawings backwards with his left hand so they could only be read in a mirror. In addition to these many drawings, he also composed and sang his own music and constructed musical instruments.

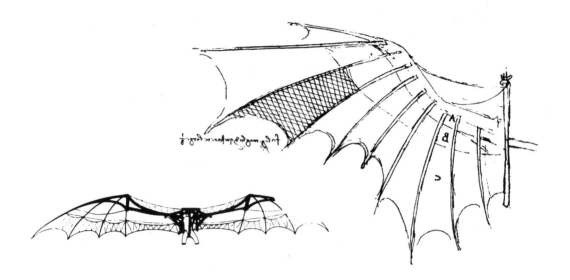

Mathematics, especially geometry and the laws governing **perspective,** perpetually fascinated Leonardo. At one time, a patron complained that Leonardo had not finished a commission, an altarpiece for a monastery, because he was spending too much time on his mathematical studies and "the sight of a brush [put] him out of temper." He utilized many of these mathematic formulas to explore perspective in drawing and painting. His desire to observe and carefully represent the visual world led Leonardo to extend the structure and depth contributed to painting by the great pre-Renaissance Italian painter Giotto, in addition to making use of his own discoveries.

The list of studies and projects Leonardo planned during his life seems endless. Unfortunately, few of these projects were actually started, fewer still were completed, and some were destroyed, notably a clay model of a huge horse—four times larger than life—which he made around 1483 as part of a statue in honor of a Milanese ruler; legend has it that the horse was so precise in detail and so powerful that it resembled a god. The patron who ordered the creation ran out of money, so the model was never cast in bronze. When the French invaded Milan in 1500, their archers used the horse for target practice and destroyed it.

Develops sfumato technique

Leonardo's surviving works are primarily drawings—over ten thousand of them—and a few paintings. These few, however, are among the most recognized and loved in all of Western art. Leonardo created a number of Madonna and child scenes for church patrons. One of the earliest was painted not long after his arrival in Milan in 1482; this work, *The Virgin of the Rocks,* provides one of the earliest examples of a Leonardo trademark: the use of sfumato or blue, misty shadows and blurred background outlines, which helps bring the figures forward and leaves the background slightly mysterious.

Leonardo left Florence for Milan in 1482. Some historians say he was discouraged about not getting enough commissions; others attribute his departure to a restlessness that kept him searching for new opportunities. In any case, Leonardo wrote a letter to the Duke of Milan recommending himself for a variety of civic projects. He offered assistance in such wartime endeavors as bridge building, cannon making, fortification of the city, and the creation of attack-resistant ships, armored cars, and catapults, and such peacetime creations as new buildings, waterways, sculpture, and painting. Leonardo was hired and spent roughly 15 years in and around Milan pursuing his typically universal array of projects.

Among his important work from this period are such portraits as *Lady with an Ermine, Portrait of a Musician,* and *La Belle Ferroniere,* all of which are noteworthy for the artist's remarkably intricate rendering of details like hair, clothing, jewelry, and even the fur of the ermine. Tiny knots, beads, curls, and lace are all delicately presented. Leonardo is also justly famous for his uncannily beautiful depictions of human skin; by using many layers of almost transparent paint, he made the flesh in his work seem to glow with an inner light and appear remarkably real. Leonardo also strove—with considerable success—to portray truthfully the personality and intelligence of each individual he painted: rather than idealizing his subjects, making them look as perfect as possible, he emphasized what was unique about each one.

Paints *The Last Supper*

In 1493 Leonardo began one of his most famous works, the **fresco** of *The Last Supper,* in the refectory (dining hall) of a convent in Milan; it took roughly three years to complete. This work has been hailed as the ultimate mark of the **Renaissance,** the highest achievement of beauty, symmetry, and spirituality. For centuries artists and art historians have written about, studied, and admired this work, not an easy task since it has deteriorated continually almost since it was painted. Leonardo's scientific zeal led him to experiment with new—and frequently unsuccessful—methods of frescoing: *The Last Supper* began crumbling, fading, and chipping during Leonardo's lifetime. Humidity, wartime destruction, and various attempts to restore it have caused further damage. Still, millions from all over the world flock to see the fresco and appreciate its significance.

Leonardo spent most of the period between 1497 and 1516 shuttling back and forth between Milan and Florence, working on a wide variety of scientific, engineering, and artistic projects. He was a member of the committee in Florence that decided where to place the giant sculpture *David* by **Michelangelo** (see

Mona Lisa (La Gioconda), 1503-05. Oil on panel, approx. 30" x 21". Louvre, Paris. Reproduced by permission of Alinari/Art Resource, NY.

entry). He also undertook some of the first geological surveys and maps of the Lombard region of Italy. From a modern standpoint, however, the crucial achievement of these years is surely the painting of his masterpiece, the *Mona Lisa*. It is probably the most famous, most visited, and most studied portrait ever painted; in fact, it often serves in popular culture as pictorial

Masterworks

1472-74	*Portrait of Ginevra de Benci*
1472-75	*Annunciation*
1483-90	*Lady with an Ermine*
1490	*Portrait of a Musician*
1490-95	*La Belle Ferroniere*
1495-97	*The Last Supper*
1503-05	*Mona Lisa (La Gioconda)*
1503-06	*Madonna of the Rocks*
1510	*Virgin and Child with St. Anne*

shorthand for the art of painting. The quiet beauty of the young woman with the slight, mysterious smile has fascinated countless viewers. Beyond her beauty, we can sense a real person with dignity, strength, and intelligence. "It does everything but speak," wrote one viewer in 1625.

In 1516 Leonardo's most important patron, Giuliano de Medici of the powerful Medici family of Florence, died. At about the same time, Leonardo received an offer from the king of France to become his "master of all arts and sciences." Leonardo was by then quite old and crippled with rheumatism, a muscle and joint disease, and thus unable to paint. Even so, he was greatly admired and pampered by the French courtiers and church officials; he lived in France for roughly two years, supervising a variety of projects before his death in 1519. Reportedly, the king of France remarked on his death that no man knew as much as had Leonardo. Aside from that clearly awed monarch, Leonardo's talent and spirit have inspired creative intellects for 500 years.

Roy Lichtenstein

Born October 27, 1923
New York, New York

R oy Lichtenstein is among a handful of artists who have become virtually synonymous with **pop art.** Since his paintings of comic strips first caused a sensation in the early 1960s, Lichtenstein has made a career of transforming images from consumer culture into gallery artifacts, challenging assumptions about "lowbrow" and "highbrow" art. Utilizing the Benday dot technique—a printing process that employs dots to create shading—he has magnified the spectacle of comics and other "throw-away" art, injecting drama and irony into a supposedly disposable form and providing a crucial early model for much of the "postmodern" art that followed.

Lichtenstein was born into a relatively prosperous New York City family. His father, Milton, owned a real estate firm. Roy graduated from Benjamin Franklin High School; though he did not study art there, he frequently painted and drew at home. Lichtenstein remembers that his father encouraged him in his artistic interests. He "thought that you should do something you

"I wanted to do things you were not supposed to do. To say you were very serious about a non-serious subject inverted everything."

▲ *Portrait: Reproduced by permission of AP/Wide World Photos.*

Kiss II, 1962.
Reproduced by
permission of
AP/Wide
World Photos.

like because you're going to spend your life doing it," the artist remarked in *ArtNews*.

After high school Lichtenstein took a summer class at New York's prestigious Art Students League; he began attending Ohio State University the subsequent fall. It was one of the few colleges at the time that offered a course in studio art. Lichtenstein's studies were interrupted by the outbreak of World War II, during which he served three years drawing maps for the Allied invasion of Germany. He returned to Ohio State in 1946 and finished his bachelor's degree, going on to obtain his master's in 1949. That year he wed his first wife, Isabel Wilson; they were married 20 years and had two sons.

Experimented with cartoons to entertain sons

During the 1950s Lichtenstein held a variety of jobs to support himself and his family, working on art projects during his free time. Among other occupations, he designed window displays, worked for graphics and engineering companies, and taught art at several universities. During this period Lichtenstein's work shared some elements of **abstract** painting, which generally dispenses with an external subject to focus instead on the interplay of values like color and texture in order to express some emotional truth. Lichtenstein borrowed attributes of this stylistic mode, but he re-introduced a subject, often "cowboys and Indians" and other generic scenes from the American West. Lichtenstein was unsatisfied with this approach, however, and spent the ensuing years in search of an appropriate style. After his sons were born in the mid-1950s, he began to experiment with painting and drawing cartoons to entertain them.

In 1960 Lichtenstein began teaching at Douglass College, part of Rutgers University in New Jersey. Due in part to the influence of several artists he met at the time, he began using ideas from his cartoons. He also found inspiration in comic strips and bubble gum wrappers, sometimes blowing them up to see what they would look like in this exaggerated form. Other artists of the time, most notably **Andy Warhol** (see entry), were also beginning to use images from consumer culture in their work. Lichtenstein was intrigued by these subjects and developed a totally new technique to present them.

Lichtenstein's basic mode has changed very little since he developed and perfected it in the early 1960s. It consists of three primary elements: thick, black borders defining objects and figures in order to emphasize the flatness of the space contained by them, brilliant—sometimes even lurid—primary colors, and the use of the Benday dot, a technique used in printing. It was named after Benjamin Day, a printer who developed this method of drafting dots of various sizes to indicate shading in printed pictures. Varying the amount of space between the points makes areas appear dark or light; the dots are printed on a printing press through screens or stencils with holes punched in them.

Used dot method to make art of "trash"

Lichtenstein particularly liked the mechanical look of the Benday system, though he did not use it mechanically. Instead, his dots were painted on by hand through the screen, sometimes with a toothbrush. Lichtenstein's desire was to approximate the look of commercially printed art. "The technique," wrote Lichtenstein, "since it was taken from printing, tells you that this is a picture of a picture, a reproduction." This was a new twist on the recurring question of what constitutes art; Lichtenstein had actually disguised the "authentic" medium of painting as the supposedly less valuable reproduction. He later attested that this approach "turned out to be so interesting that eventually it became impossible for me to do any other kind of painting."

The first such work to gain Lichtenstein substantial attention was *Look Mickey!,* which depicts cartoon characters Mickey Mouse and Donald Duck fishing on a dock. Of course, critics objected that cartoons were not serious art and thus did not deserve a place in galleries and museums. But others realized that Lichtenstein was commenting on the widespread images of popular culture familiar to everyone, just as paintings of Greek gods would have been familiar to mainstream audiences of the past. Many found Lichtenstein's subject matter a breath of fresh air in contrast to the often somber and highly intellectual style of **abstract expressionism,** which had come to dominate the art world in the 1950s.

In 1961 and 1962 Lichtenstein perfected his technique, making the dots larger and line and color crisper. He studied other subjects, such as advertising images from newspapers, the telephone directory, and even restaurant menus; rather than copy the images, he reproduced them in his own style. He also borrowed scenes from popular comic strips—especially romance comics—and painted them complete with speech bubbles. Some of his most familiar works portray worried young women wondering aloud about their love lives. Lichtenstein also painted war scenes, inspired by a mixture of his own experiences, comics, and the popular war movies of the 1940s and 1950s. One of his most famous works, *Blam!,* features a fighter plane exploding and twisting in the air. Lichtenstein commented, "I like to

make explosions into elaborate beautiful forms, which is what they become in a comic strip." This was the first time a painter had used modern wartime technology as a subject.

As the 1960s progressed Lichtenstein applied his style to several other scenes, including landscapes and sunsets. In *Sinking Sun,* he painted the sun descending beneath a large cloud formation, around which its rays shine. But, according to the artist, this was not a "real" landscape. In Lichtenstein's words,

Roy Lichtenstein

Pop Art: Elevating "Trash" Culture

Pop art developed from two basic concepts: one was the exploration of the post-World War II consumer society through imitation of the kind of images used in advertising, packaging, and the media; the other was a reaction to what pop art practitioners considered the overly serious and theoretical nature of the style known as **abstract expressionism,** which dominated the art world of the 1950s. The fusion of these concerns—both of which implied a turning away from abstract expressionism's self-involvement—allowed the images saturating everyday life onto canvases and into museums. Naturally, the idea that cartoon ducks and soap advertisements were appropriate subject matter for "fine art" generated controversy; it also expanded the borders of the fundamental argument over what constitutes art.

Early examples of the new style began popping up in the mid-1950s, especially in New York and London. Still, no single style defined pop art; it varied—from paintings of targets and flags by Jasper Johns, to the "combine paintings" or **collages** of Robert Rauschenberg. This invigorating mood emerged in art at about the same time that rock and roll was gaining popularity. By the time Elvis Presley was at his height and the Beatles hit the scene in 1963, pop art was rocking the art world, mirroring the brashness and exuberance of what conservatives were decrying as "the devil's music." Landmark works of pop art include the Brillo boxes and Campbell's Soup cans of **Andy Warhol** (see entry), Roy Lichtenstein's paintings of comic strips, and Claes Oldenburg's cakes made of plaster and soft sculptures of telephones and toilets. These artists took the most familiar images imag-

"It gives you the idea of landscape. But ... it's far from reality, as artificial as it can be. It's telling you that you are looking at something beautiful, even though you know you are not. On the other hand, maybe you are." In fact, the unreliability of a painting, the mixed message of beauty and fakery—as opposed to the older ideal of the artwork as a window onto a beautiful world—is a staple of contemporary artistic thought.

Mocking and paying tribute

Lichtenstein has also on occasion "copied" paintings by well-known artists, taking figures or scenes painted by **Pablo Picasso, Henri Matisse, Piet Mondrian** (see entries), and oth-

inable as their subjects: detergent boxes, beer cans, and hot dogs, or flashy images of movie stars and presidents.

The character of pop art was frequently witty and humorous; it mocked the seriousness of art critics and gallery owners who had segregated art from the real world and its ordinary citizenry. Pop advocates objected to the transformation of the art world into a highly specialized field dominated by "experts" and the rich. Innovators like Warhol and Lichtenstein made their creations resemble printed works that could be easily reproduced, rather than expensive, precious objects. Critics were outraged; one wrote that "art galleries are being invaded by the pinheaded and contemptible style of gumchewers, Bobby-soxers and, worse, delinquents." Vast numbers of museum visitors, however, were relieved that artists were again producing works they could understand and enjoy. And enjoyment—after the somber reign of the abstract expressionists—seemed positively revolutionary.

Some later pop artists did address serious issues, commenting on poverty, war, inequality, pollution, and materialism. They often tried to make their points with shock tactics, as did Andy Warhol with his cool, impersonal images of car wrecks and electric chairs. But these methods differed radically from the playful parodies usually associated with pop art. "Just as the impressionists recorded street life in turn-of-the-century Paris," noted one observer, "the pop artists provided an instant chronicle of what mattered most to people in the sixties and seventies."

ers and adapting them to his comic-strip style. One of his most famous copies is of the series of paintings of the cathedral in Rouen, France, by **Claude Monet** (see entry). Monet helped pioneer the nineteenth-century style called **impressionism.** In this manner he painted several views of the cathedral to show how the shifting sunlight changed the scene's appearance. Lichtenstein painted his five views of the church using his dot and stencil method to make "a mechanical representation of Impressionism." In such efforts, he is at once mocking these old masters and paying tribute to them.

Lichtenstein also parodied abstract expressionism in his brush stroke paintings of the mid-1960s. The very act of using a brush to apply paint with a stroke was crucially important to the ideas behind abstract expressionism. Lichtenstein made fun of such grandiose theories by painting cartoon-like images of brush strokes. He wrote, "It amused me that the brushstrokes I made were actually fake and tediously drawn out rather than being brushstrokes at all." Lichtenstein also applied this spirit to paintings of architectural monuments like the pyramids of Egypt and ruins of ancient Greek temples.

In the 1970s Lichtenstein again turned to new themes, among them "mirrors"—actually round and oval canvases with areas of solid color and dots. His *Self-portrait* of 1978 presents the shoulder area of a T-shirt above which, where the head should be, is a mirror; this playful flimflam was inspired by a painting by the surrealist painter René Magritte. Lichtenstein also painted **still lifes** in various modern styles during the decade.

The 1980s and 1990s brought more change to Lichtenstein's work. Several paintings of the period combine his cartoon style with the ideas of abstract expressionism. In *Two Paintings: Radiator and Folded Sheets,* he displays a pair of compositions hung side by side on a wall of which the viewer sees only a portion. One composition, the radiator, is rendered in a style resembling 1950s abstract art, while the other, the folded sheets, is represented in his recognizable comic-strip style.

This painting of two paintings hanging on a wall—the section of wall actually the canvas itself—emphasizes Lichtenstein's desire to make viewers question his medium. Which portion of this illusion is "real?" Yet even as he poses these challenges, Lichtenstein retains his characteristic humor and sense of the absurd. Perhaps more ironically, reproductions of his most familiar cartoon works have themselves been embraced by the consumer culture, appearing on everything from greeting cards to billboards.

Maya Lin

Born October 5, 1959
Athens, Ohio

A t the tender age of 21 Maya Lin became one of the most controversial artists in the United States. Her design for the Vietnam Veterans Memorial in Washington, D.C., came under attack for a variety of reasons, but it would eventually become the most visited monument in the country. Lin has worked on numerous public and private projects since then. Each has been praised for her creative and expressive treatment of the subject depicted. Some have also been severely criticized and even vandalized. Lin's ability to blend sculpture and architecture has earned her a reputation as one of the most innovative artists working today.

Maya Ying Lin grew up in Athens, Ohio, where her parents were on the faculty of Ohio University. Her father, Henry Lin, was dean of the art school and a ceramic artist. Her mother, Julia Lin, was a poet and professor of Asian and English literature. Both immigrated to the United States from China. Early on Lin displayed a talent for mathematics and art. She was a

"I love architecture and I love sculpture, but I could never choose. Sculpture to me is like poetry, and architecture is like prose."

top-notch student and after high school was accepted to Yale University in Connecticut.

At Yale she was informed by her professors that she could study either sculpture or architecture, but not both. Lin admits that while she was officially a student in the architecture school, she used to sneak over to the art school to take sculpture classes. This double interest has been a curse and a blessing throughout Lin's career. "There's an incredible suspicion that if you're interested in two different disciplines, then you treat them lightly ... but I could never choose," she has said. Indeed, Lin's natural gifts and training in both fields contribute to the unique nature of her work.

Stirs controversy with Vietnam Veterans Memorial

In October 1980 an organization called the Vietnam Veterans Memorial Fund announced it would sponsor a nationwide competition to design a memorial honoring those who had served in the Vietnam War. Nearly 1,500 aspiring artists submitted proposals. A panel of distinguished judges, including architects, sculptors, and landscape architects, chose the final design: a simple V-shaped wall of polished black stone inscribed with the names of the roughly 58,000 men and women who were killed in the war or declared missing in action. The designer was a senior architecture student at Yale named Maya Lin—and a total unknown in the art world.

Soon after Lin's concept was approved by the appropriate government agencies, a group of veterans began to protest the design. Their leader called the wall a "black gash of shame" and said it was insulting to the memory of those who had died. They wanted a traditional white marble sculpture featuring figures of soldiers. This group even attacked Lin herself with sexist and racist slurs. The debate over the memorial—which mirrored the larger issue of unresolved national pain lingering from the war era and the treatment and dire circumstance of many of its veterans—raged for almost a year, with veterans, writers, artists, and the public weighing in with their opinions. A compromise was finally reached: a traditional monument would be installed near the entrance of the site to the memorial wall.

The experience made Lin angry and bitter. She detested the publicity and pressure surrounding the situation. After completing the project, she hoped to return to being just another student. She began graduate studies in architecture at Harvard University but then left school to try and recapture her anonymity. She took a position working for an architect in Boston. During this time Lin's disillusionment was turned around by an unexpected development: the Vietnam Veterans Memorial quickly became one of the most highly respected works of art—and the most visited public monument—in the country.

Demonstrates gift for involving viewers

Lin had created an environment capable of moving visitors to great emotion. Thousands of veterans, surviving family members, and others came to find the names of loved ones and left behind flowers and other mementos. Lin had found a perfect formula for involving people directly in the work and, in the process, had heightened for many the experience of honoring and grieving for the dead. Somehow her efforts had managed to help heal the deep psychic wounds inflicted on America by the Vietnam War. Indeed, so many visitors have touched the wall, many leaving with rubbings of the engraved names, that by 1994 restoration had begun to repair cracks and other wear associated with the constant attention.

In creating her works Lin devotes herself to a serious process of study. For the Vietnam Veterans Memorial, she carefully examined the area in which the wall was to be built, taking into consideration the slope of the land and the adjacent structures. She also investigated the art of other eras and cultures to see how memorials honoring the dead had been conceived throughout history. Moreover, she read the journals of soldiers from World War I.

For her next project, a memorial for the civil rights movement in Montgomery, Alabama, Lin studied the history of the movement and the writings of Martin Luther King, Jr. It was in his writings that she found the inspiration for this monument: one of King's favorite phrases from the Bible, which he used in his famous "I Have a Dream" speech. King insisted that seekers of equality would not be satisfied until "justice rolls down like waters and righteousness like a mighty stream." The image of water rolling down inspired Lin.

Water rolls in Montgomery

The design for this monument, which was dedicated in 1989, was a large, solid granite disk engraved with the names and events of the civil rights movement of the 1950s and 1960s. Behind the disk is a nine-foot granite wall inscribed with the quotation from King. Both pieces are covered with a thin veil of constantly running water. Visitors are attracted to the water, through which they can trace the inscriptions with their fingers. Lin explained, "I'm trying to make people become involved with the piece on all levels, with the touch and sound of the water, with the words, with

the memories." The Montgomery monument has been praised for capturing "the essence of a moment of history with simple forms that evoke the widest range of emotions."

During the 1990s Lin has been involved with many projects, including eight public commissions. She has renovated two floors of a building in New York City for a new Museum of African Art. She has designed a private home in California and a large earthwork in front of an aerospace company building in Michigan. Another great honor came Lin's way when she was asked by Yale to create a sculpture to commemorate women at the university. She designed a three-foot-high table of green granite. A funnel-shaped hole in the table allows water to seep through. On top is a spiral of numbers, which begin with zero and run into the thousands, indicating the number of women who have attended Yale over the years. *The Women's Table* stands in front of the university's Sterling Memorial Library. In 1994 Lin designed a 14-foot-long clock for New York's Pennsylvania Station. It is made of translucent glass, lighted by hundreds of fiber optic light points. According to *Newsweek,* it hovers above the heads of travelers "like a glowing flying saucer."

In 1993 Lin created a sculptural landscape work called *Groundswell* at Ohio State University—a three-level garden of crushed green glass. For this project, Lin directed a crew of six as 40 tons of recycled glass were hoisted by a crane into a cone-shaped sifter. The glass was "poured" into soft mounds to create a wave effect. Like this one, many of Lin's works reveal her concern with the environment. She often uses stone, water, earth, and, as in *Groundswell,* recycled materials. This work has received some criticism, and a vandal poured red paint onto a portion of the glass, forcing Lin to replace 14 tons of it. Lin has not become immune to the controversies her work continues to inspire. "I've learned to expect criticism," she told the *New York Times,* "but it still hurts."

Lin devotes considerable time to overseeing the many details and finishing touches of each of her works. When not on-site, she works in an office, a nondescript room in an old building in New York, or in a house she owns in Vermont, where she creates her abstract or nonrepresentational sculptural pieces. Having endured such harsh reactions to her work, Lin stays out of the public eye as much as possible. Still, so much of her work is so public and so innovative that publicity is hard to avoid. Much of the debate centering on her efforts comes from the difficulty people have in categorizing them as architecture or sculpture. Lin has seemed to take advantage of this confusion as she continues to create the unexpected in hope that she will further involve and move those who view her work.

Edouard Manet

Born January 23, 1832
Paris, France

Died April 30, 1883
Paris, France

"There is only one true thing: instantly paint what you see. When you've got it, you've got it. When you haven't, you begin again. All the rest is humbug."

Art historians may dispute the contention that Edouard Manet was the father of modern art, but few will deny that he played a vital role in the stylistic upheavals that led to its birth in the mid-nineteenth century. Manet was not a typical revolutionary. Though he led a conservative life with respect to social custom, he rejected the traditions of the formal art world and ultimately helped to turn that universe upside down. Manet advanced the very modern view that artists had a responsibility to tell the truth in their work—whether that truth was beautiful or ugly. He met with constant criticism and abuse during his career but clung stubbornly to his forward-looking view of art's mission.

Manet was raised in an affluent, cultured home in Paris. His father, August Manet, was a lawyer who worked for the French Ministry of Justice and later became a judge. A stern man who lived by a strict routine, the senior Manet had determined that Edouard, too, would be a lawyer. Manet's mother,

Eugénie Fournier Manet, was very different from her husband. She had grown up in a sophisticated, worldly home and possessed great artistic and musical talents. She encouraged Edouard in his art, though considering her husband's feelings on the matter, such encouragement was most likely kept secret.

◀ *Portrait (p. 272): Reproduced by permission of The Bettmann Archive.*

Resists traditional education

Manet detested the local schools he attended; his poor grades would perhaps have hastened his forcible departure from these institutions had his father not been so influential. Monsieur Manet refused to pay an extra fee so his son could attend an art class at the high school, but the boy's fortunes changed when his uncle provided the necessary funds. It must have taken courage for the 16-year-old Manet to announce to his father that he wanted to become a painter. This was not considered a reputable career, but since he seemed strongly disinclined to study law, the family pressured young Manet to become a naval officer. He spent six months on a ship sailing to Brazil and found it no less tedious than school; he failed the naval academy examination twice.

At that time art in France was ruled by the Institut de France, the government's department of culture. **Academic art** was dominated by standards of beauty and grandeur that derived from ancient Greek and Roman culture; these centuries-old traditions and the limited scope of approved subjects—generally figures from classical mythology and the Bible—formed a climate that more adventurous artists found stifling. Nonetheless, any artist who hoped to be successful had to submit to such standards and enter works in the yearly **salons,** exhibitions arranged by the government and judged by members of the Institut's Ecole des Beaux Arts, or school of fine arts. Manet finally prevailed over his father's objections, and in 1850 he was allowed to enter art school, though not the Ecole des Beaux Arts, as his father wished. Instead he entered the school of a well-known painter, Thomas Couture.

Manet disliked the academic style from the beginning and insisted on drawing the models who posed for his class as they really looked, rather than refining his depictions to fit the classical standard of beauty and proportion. Sometimes he shocked the instructor by drawing clothes on the model and putting a cigarette between the sitter's fingers or a beer glass in the model's hand, rather than portraying an idealized pose from ancient statuary. Although Manet loved art and possessed the essential painterly skills, he also reveled in modern life and longed to put it on canvas. Paris in the 1850s teemed with precisely the sort of vitality he sought to memorialize; Manet often wandered through the city with his sketchbook, drawing whatever struck his fancy. He argued constantly with his teacher about art and modernity. Few artists had tackled subjects that were not noble, heroic, or historical, just ordinary and immediate.

Resists constraints of "academic" style

Dutch portrait painter **Rembrandt van Rijn,** Spanish court painter **Francisco Goya** (see entries), and French caricaturist Honoré Daumier may have provided some inspiration for Manet in this respect, but he had few predecessors in his quest to take painting out of the conservative tradition of the salon and into the street. Even after a trip to Italy in 1853, where he viewed and copied the works of the masters **Michelangelo** and **Titian** (see entries), Manet could not accept the constraints of the academic style.

Spanish art and culture enjoyed considerable popularity in France during this time, and the work of seventeenth-century court painter **Diego Velazquez** (see entry) strongly influenced Manet, particularly the Spanish master's colors and spatial structure. The opening of Japan to the West in the mid-nineteenth century brought Japanese woodblock prints to Europe; radical French painters, Manet included, found them especially compelling. Manet experimented in his drawings and **etchings** with the flat space and heavy black outlines typical of these **woodcuts.** A third important influence on Manet was that most modern of all inventions—photography. When Louis Daguerre announced his new invention in Paris in 1839, he created a sensation. To young artists like Manet, this astonishing technology provided a new window on the world. One of the most famous photographers of the time, Paul Nadar, was a close friend of Manet; he joined the painter's circle of artists and writers who gathered at the Paris cafés.

The first painting Manet submitted to the Paris Salon, 1859's *The Absinthe Drinker,* challenged virtually every tenet of the academic philosophy. He used a street-dweller he knew as the model for this portrait of a drunken vagrant. Employing a sharply limited range of colors, mostly browns and blacks, Manet posed the figure against a wall with a vague background. This "unpleasant" person in an "ugly" setting was of course rejected by the salon jury, as were many of Manet's paintings over the years. During this period he painted a variety of works with popular Spanish themes, such as *The Dead Toreador,* and portraits of street people like *The Street Singer.* Despite the familiar subjects—which were in themselves outside the norm—his unusual use of color, flat spaces, dark outlines, and frequently disorienting representations eluded the understanding of both the art establishment and the general public. Traditional **perspective,** with its proportionate views of figures and landscapes properly receding into the distance, had been the standard since pre-Renaissance Italian fresco artist Giotto and multitalented Renaissance master **Leonardo da Vinci** (see entry). Viewers felt threatened by Manet's paintings, which seemed to jump off the canvas at them.

Shocks with *Déjeuner sur l'herbe*

The year 1863 was pivotal for Manet. He gained considerable fame—though of the least desirable sort—thanks to an audacious work that would eventually be considered a masterpiece. The painting, which he submitted to the salon that year, provoked responses ranging from wild laughter to complete outrage. *Le Déjeuner sur l'herbe (Luncheon on the Grass)* depicts a forest setting with a woman and two men gathered around a picnic. Manet borrowed directly from sixteenth-century Italian drawings for these figures. Nothing would have been shocking about this except that the men are dressed in fashionable contemporary attire, while the woman is nude and gazes directly—and provocatively—at the viewer.

In *Le Déjeuner,* Manet seemed to be toying with his audience by setting up the kind of traditional scene they might expect,

Le Déjeuner sur l'herbe, 1863. Approx. 7' x 8'10". Galerie du Jeu de Paume, Paris. Reproduced by permission of Scala/Art Resource, NY.

then overturning those expectations. Rather than present his nude female subject in the unadorned classical tradition, he depicted what might be the "behind-the-scenes" view of nude portraiture, with all of its sexual, and economic, implications; Manet exposed the reality that for all its lofty ideals, the academic style necessitated that male artists pay female models—real women, not goddesses or biblical figures—to take off their clothes. Thus he not only introduced a modern element into a traditional scene but also used this pastoral setting to taunt the respectable art world with its own hidden truths. It was a successful scandal, thanks in large part to the disapproval—institutional and otherwise—that greeted such a revolutionary gesture. Manet could no longer be ignored.

These years were comfortable for Manet personally and socially, though much of the criticism he received rankled him.

Despite his reputation as an artistic rebel, he desired social approval and was known for his gentlemanly dress and manners. In 1863, a year after his father's death, he married his mistress, Suzanne Leenhoff. He had been supporting her and her son—it is unclear whether or not the child was his—for roughly ten years; the boy appears in several paintings. The family, often including Manet's mother, spent summers in the country, where Manet painted local scenes. In Paris, however, he became the leader of a group of young artists and writers who rejected academic painting and sought a modern vision. Among these were **Pierre-Auguste Renoir, Claude Monet, Paul Cézanne** (see entries), Edgar Degas, Camille Pissarro, and Henri Fantin-Latour. They engaged in passionate discussions in cafés and in Manet's studio and eventually became the core of the **impressionist** movement.

Tweaks art establishment anew

Manet continued his innovations in color, space, and outline despite persistent criticism, waiting only two years before shocking the art world once more. In 1865 he presented his *Olympia,* again a variation on a traditional theme. Paintings by Titian and Goya were direct models for this reclining nude, but as in *Le Déjeuner,* Manet's female subject was no Greek goddess; she was a familiar Parisian courtesan, or prostitute, depicted lounging on the luxurious embroidered sheets of her bed. Her nudity is not the ideal, modest beauty familiar to viewers of Manet's day, and she is not demurely gazing into the distance or shading her eyes. She instead occupies the foreground, completely exposed, brazenly meeting the viewer's gaze. Manet presents her with a ribbon choker around her neck, a bracelet at her wrist, her feet in fancy slippers, and a flower in her hair, all underscoring the casual shamelessness of her nudity. She's paying no attention to the servant bringing her a bouquet of flowers, presumably from some gentleman caller. This modern woman is almost pushed into the viewer's face by the lack of space behind her; only the patterned wallpaper offers a clue about the setting. It is difficult for contemporary viewers to imagine the outrage the work provoked in 1865. It was called wicked, shocking, and ugly. Manet knew it was immediate and real.

Bar at the Folies-Bergère,
*1882. Oil on canvas,
37" x 51". Courtauld
Institute Galleries, London.*

In the late 1860s and into the 1870s, Manet's works adopted some new elements, partly as a result of his friendship with painters like Berthe Morisot—who became his sister-in-law—Degas, and Monet. During their summers in the countryside around Paris, these painters set up their easels outdoors and tried to capture the vivid sunlight, brilliantly colored clothing, and rich vegetation they saw. Such works as *Boating, Claude Monet in His Floating Studio,* and *Argenteuil* display Manet's utter departure from the academic tradition, with his loose brush strokes, intimate sense of space, and, most particularly, modern subject matter.

In 1875 Manet developed a debilitating disease, a slow deterioration of the central nervous system, which made it increasingly difficult for him to paint; he turned to smaller works and more flexible media like pastels and watercolors. His last large painting, *Bar at the Folies-Bergère,* was the most complete synthesis of his work and philosophy. It is a powerful "snapshot" of a barmaid, with all the liveliness of the bar reflected in a mirror behind her. The totality of Manet's style is evident—the immediacy of the moment depicted, the complicated space, the expressive brush strokes. Numerous attributes of this work have become defining characteristics of modern art.

After Manet's death at the age of 51, his colleagues continued the revolution he had begun, bringing to fruition the impressionist project so familiar now in the modern visions of Dutch painter **Vincent van Gogh,** French "pointillist" **Georges Seurat,** and French painter **Paul Gauguin** (see entries), among countless others. Cézanne declared that Manet's *Olympia* began a new renaissance in painting, and Degas maintained that Manet was "greater than we thought." The work of this artistic revolutionary remains vibrant and challenging, both within and without its historical context.

Masterworks

1861	*The Old Musician*
1862	*The Street Singer*
	Lola de Valence
1863	*Le Déjeuner sur l'herbe (Luncheon on the Grass)*
	Dead Toreador
	Olympia
1864	*Races at Longchamp*
1866	*The Fifer*
1868	*Portrait of Émile Zola*
	The Balcony
1873	*The Railway*
1878	*The Road-Menders in the Rue de Berne*
1882	*Bar at the Folies-Bergère*

Man Ray

Born August 27, 1890
Philadelphia, Pennsylvania
Died November 18, 1976
Paris, France

"You can say that I'm a retired banjo player, or a former chewing gum executive, or a retired coal dealer. It doesn't matter about me; the important thing is my painting."

Man Ray's work—in painting, photography, sculpture, assemblage, and film—is among the most surprising and shocking of the modern era. In addition to pushing the creative envelope, he also made many technical advances in the use of photography; one such process was named the Rayograph in his honor. Mysterious, witty, and erotic, his creations embody the challenge to institutional art that was characterized by the styles known as **surrealism** and **dadaism**.

The son of Russian immigrants, Man Ray was born Emmanuel Rudnitsky, but after his family gave him the nickname Man Ray he never used any other. The Rudnitsky clan moved from Philadelphia to Brooklyn, New York, when Man Ray was seven. Man Ray displayed an interest in art from an early age and once made a drawing of the battleship *Maine* using every color in his box of crayons. In his autobiography, *Self Portrait*, he related that he paid little attention to his formal schoolwork and spent most of his time painting and drawing.

After graduating from high school, he was offered a scholarship to study architecture.

◀ *Portrait* (p. 280): *Reproduced by permission of Archive Photos.*

Exposed to cubism and African art

But what he wanted was to paint, so he held odd jobs to support himself while he pursued his vocation. Man Ray also attended life drawing classes in the evenings and haunted the galleries and museums of New York. It was at the famous Gallery 291 run by **Alfred Stieglitz** (see entry) that he became familiar with works by modern American and European painters and photographers such as the Spaniard **Pablo Picasso,** Frenchman **Paul Cézanne** (see entries), and American George Bellows. Works in styles previously unseen in domestic galleries, including the fruits of **cubism** and African art, were on view there.

Man Ray's first important work, *Tapestry,* bears the stamp of these influences. He made the cloth construction in 1911 from samples obtained from a tailor's shop; the resulting patchwork strongly resembles some of the cubist paintings he had seen. Already he had established his trademark use of unusual materials. It was around this time that he met the French artist **Marcel Duchamp** (see entry), who became his closest friend. Duchamp, Man Ray, and artist Francis Picabia would be pioneers in America of a movement known as dadaism, which had begun in Switzerland. Dada was based on a perception of life's essentially irrational and absurd character and challenged the idea that there existed laws of beauty or organization in art. Dada artists worked to shock, surprise, and disorient their audiences through the use of bizarre combinations, disturbing images, and dream logic.

Another important influence on Man Ray's art during this time was the famous 1913 New York art exhibition known as the Armory Show, which included works in a variety of modern—and controversial—styles. Many of these creations were attacked as scandalous by critics and conventional artists. The impact of the show on artists like Man Ray was enormous; it encouraged him to continue experimenting with cubism and with "anti-artistic" works. In 1914, Man Ray married Adon Lacroiz, and his first solo show took place in New York in 1915. A Chicago collector was sufficiently impressed by Man Ray's work to purchase six paintings for $2,000, a substantial amount for the time. This was enough for Man Ray to buy his own studio.

Makes waves with strange self-portrait

Between 1916 and 1921 Man Ray worked feverishly in the dada and cubist styles. His most renowned creation from this phase is most likely *The Rope Dancer Accompanies Herself with Her Shadows,* a work that combined painting and paper cutouts. He also undertook a "self-portrait" in 1917; in the words of the *New York Times,* it "consisted of two nonringing electric bells and a push button attached to a background of aluminum and black paint that bore at its center an imprint of his hand." Needless to say, identifying this odd artifact as a self-portrait challenged a slew of prevailing notions about representation. Man Ray was also among the earliest practitioners of a process known as assemblage. Assemblages are works assembled, or put together, from items of varying media, often found objects. Though Man Ray's compositional skills are evident in these works, they were revolutionary in the context of mainstream art.

When Man Ray was 31 years old, he moved to Paris and was immediately accepted there into the circle of artists working in the dada movement. He continued painting and creating assemblages, as well as producing sculpture and **collages,** which, like assemblage, incorporates various kinds of materials but generally involves a framed surface. Man Ray soon realized that he could not earn a living from his paintings, so he began earning money by photographing fashion layouts and portraits of prominent society people. He had begun teaching himself photography in order to take pictures of his own art works, but he soon developed such skill in this imcreasingly popular medium

Man Ray sits on May 20, 1964 among some of his art objects, ▶
including (from left) **Main Ray, The Gift,** *and* **Person to Person;**
the pipe and the glass soap bubble he is "blowing" is titled
What We All Lack. *Reproduced by permission of UPI/Bettmann.*

that other artists began to hire him to photograph their creations. He achieved fame for photographing some of the most important art figures of the day, including American writers Gertrude Stein and Ernest Hemingway, Irish writer James Joyce, and Picasso. Man Ray gained a reputation for unusual poses that nonetheless revealed the personality of his subject.

The 1920s and 1930s were phenomenally successful and busy years for Man Ray, years that saw his involvement in the artistic movement called surrealism. He also made several films and even appeared in one by director René Clair. Most importantly, he continued to hone his distinctive, humorously creative perspective. Once he found a broken lamp from which he removed the shade, cutting it to form a spiral. And one of his most famous assemblages was made from an iron. He glued tacks on the flat bottom of the iron; by depriving it of its functionality, he transformed it into an aesthetic object, absurd and menacing, that he called *The Gift.* Another infamous work from this time, *Indestructible Object,* consisted of a metronome to which Man Ray attached a photograph of a human eye. The eye would swing back and forth on the metronome's arm as the device ticked. These works are considered the forerunners of the **pop art** of the 1960s.

Innovates in photography

In Paris, while pursuing photography, Man Ray discovered a new process: he accidentally placed some objects, including a funnel and a thermometer, onto unexposed photographic paper. He was delighted when, on turning on the light, he found that white silhouettes of these objects had "printed" on the black background. He experimented for many years with this process, which he called the Rayograph, and with a reverse process called solarization. He often called this "painting with light." His Rayographs and other photographic works were exhibited around the world and appeared in numerous publications.

Violon d'Ingres, *1923.* © *1995 Artists Rights Society (ARS), New* ▶ *York/ADAGP/Man Ray Trust, Paris. Giraudon/Art Resource, NY.*

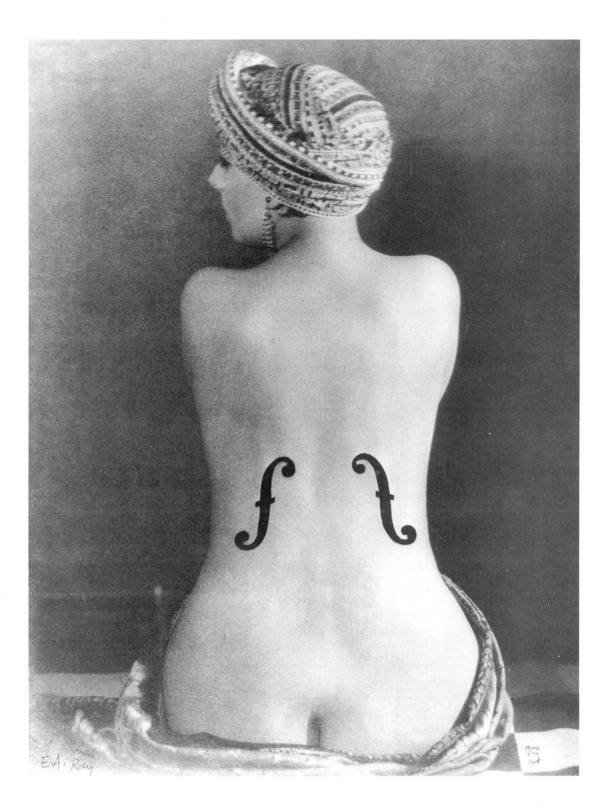

Dada

The movement known as dadaism comprised a total challenge to traditional concepts of art. Indeed, dadaists called their works "anti-art." They attacked everything that mainstream culture held sacred—from literature and art to government and religion—to demonstrate their disgust with social conformity and institutions of power.

Dadaism began in Zurich, Switzerland, in 1916. The first members of the movement were artists and writers who gathered at the Cabaret Voltaire, run by poet Hugo Ball and singer Emmy Hemmings. The entertainment presented at the club attracted a sizable group of young people who felt disillusioned about society and horrified by the slaughter of World War I, which was raging at the time. Ball and Hemmings were joined by poet Tristan Tzara, who is considered the real founder of dadaism. He even chose the movement's name, claiming to have picked it out of a dictionary at random. "Dada" is the French word for a child's hobbyhorse.

The shows at the cabaret included bizarre and aggressive performances of music, poetry, and theater. The dadaists wanted to shock the audience, to make observers recognize the insanity that surrounded them. Tzara claimed there were no theories of dada art, just the idea of protest. He was a genius at attracting publicity and ensured that the dadaists generated maximum controversy. The conservative press attacked dadaism as dangerous, their warnings fueled in large part by false information fed to them by Tzara. Once he announced that the dadaists were sponsoring a lecture by the popular actor Charlie Chaplin. Reporters and hundreds of people

Man Ray's most famous photograph of these years in Paris is called *Violon d'Ingres.* It is a picture of a woman's back on which Man Ray painted the sound holes of a violin. This work—spoofing a painting by the nineteenth-century French artist Ingres—at once jibes playfully at the "serious" art world and exemplifies the dreamlike eroticism of the surrealists, which often involved mysterious transformations of the female nude.

After 20 years in France, Man Ray returned to the United States during the Nazi occupation of Paris in the early 1940s. He settled in Hollywood, where he worked and taught for roughly ten years. Man Ray's works were collected and displayed in

showed up only to find out that there was no lecture. It was merely another dada trick.

The dada movement spread quickly to major cities in Europe, especially throughout Paris. Several journals were published to spread dadaist ideas, which were, of course, largely flexible and self-contradictory. These publications included works by prominent writers and poets, as well as drawings by several of the century's most daring artists. Some of the important artists associated with dada were Jean Arp, Sophie Taeuber, Marcel Janco, Kurt Schwitters, and Max Ernst. Although he was never formally part of the dada group, the Frenchman **Marcel Duchamp** (see entry) was considered the earliest supporter of dadaism. His "Readymades" had stirred up the art world in the years before 1916 and encouraged the movement in New York, where he lived for most of the dada heyday. He and fellow artist and friend Francis Picabia, along with Man Ray, are considered the founders of dada in the United States.

The dada movement burned itself out after just six years; Tzara himself declared it dead in 1922. But the strains of the rebellion carried into several later art movements, especially **surrealism** and **pop art.** The dadaists were perhaps simply ahead of their time, for many of their rebellious ideas were revived in the protest years of the 1960s. In fact, in 1966 the people of Zurich commemorated the fiftieth anniversary of the birth of dadaism by mounting a show to recreate the atmosphere of the original dada movement at the Cabaret Voltaire.

several exhibitions, including one in New York in 1945 titled "Objects of My Affection" that was comprised almost entirely of items the artist had found by chance. His first marriage had ended in divorce, and he married again during these years.

From the early 1950s until his death in 1976, Man Ray lived in France, working on a multitude of projects. One involved photographing the adjustable wooden figures that artists use as models, arranging them in frequently provocative poses to sometimes humorous, sometimes eerie effect. He was also one of the first artists to use the airbrush. He continued experimenting with photography, worked on several books, and helped organize exhibitions.

Masterworks

1911	*Tapestry*
1916	*The Rope Dancer Accompanies Herself with Her Shadows*
1917	*Self-Portrait*
1921	*The Gift*
1922	*Gertrude Stein with Picasso Portrait*
1923	*Violon d'Ingres*
1924	*Indestructible Object*

Man Ray maintained, according to the *New York Times,* that there were "no two things alike in [his] work and that he was constantly evolving." He won a score of awards that recognized his creativity and inventiveness, including the Legion d'Honneur, France's highest laurel. He occupied a storied place in the worlds of painting and photography, explaining that he used photography for subjects he did not wish to paint and painting for what could not be photographed. Most of all, he specialized in realizing what previously could not be imagined.

Henri Matisse

Born December 31, 1869
Le Cateau-Cambresis, France
Died November 3, 1954
Nice, France

Henri Matisse ranks among the most acclaimed and imitated of modern artists, but his innovations shocked many of his contemporaries and only gained widespread acceptance after generating substantial controversy. By the late twentieth century, however, the influence of his bold style can be observed not only in the so-called fine arts but in virtually every facet of popular culture.

Matisse was raised in northern France. His parents, Emile and Gerard Matisse, ran a kind of grocery store. Unlike many artists, he did not spend time drawing or painting as a child. He was expected to take over the family business or, with luck, become a lawyer. Matisse did study law in Paris for two years; but he unwittingly doomed his legal career when, in 1890 while working as a law clerk, he began attending early morning drawing classes meant for curtain designers. While recovering from appendicitis that year, Matisse received a box of paints from his

"What I dream of is an art of balance, of purity and serenity devoid of troubling or depressing subject matter."

▲ *Portrait: Reproduced by permission of AP/Wide World Photos.*

mother and soon thereafter decided to pursue a career in art. He was 20 years old.

Experiments with various styles

Matisse studied for several years in Paris with traditional painters. To earn money he made copies of famous works at the French national museum, the Louvre. At the time Paris was the center of a revolution in the visual arts. Besides **impressionism,** other new ideas were being introduced by painters like Frenchmen **Paul Cézanne** and **Georges Seurat** and **Vincent van Gogh** of the Netherlands. At the Louvre Matisse was attracted to the passion of Spanish artist **Francisco Goya.** He also admired the work of his countryman **Henri Toulouse-Lautrec** (see entries) and, like numerous artists of the time, was fascinated by the woodblock prints of Japan. Matisse experimented with ideas from all these sources; by 1897 he was on his way to finding his own style.

The first results of his experimentation were revealed in 1898 when he painted a male nude—not in the usual flesh tones, but all in blue. This unorthodox choice reflected his conviction that color should be used to express emotion. By 1905 Matisse had become the leader of a group of artists called "Les Fauves," the wild beasts, after their exhibit shocked the public. **Fauvism,** as their style became known, is characterized by broad strokes of very bright, often clashing color. The heightened hues and dark borders defining shapes invested their work with tremendous energy. A noteworthy example from this time is Matisse's *Woman with the Hat,* a portrait of the artist's wife, Amelie Parayre—whom he'd married in 1899—in a very large *chapeau.* Although compositionally a traditional rendering of an elegant lady, the painting's use of color—the dress, hat, and even the face are painted in patches of green, red, orange, and blue—was scandalous for the time. Matisse gained some fame when American writer Gertrude Stein and her brother Michael Stein bought the painting. Over the years, the two bought many of his works.

Except for the Steins, however, Matisse attracted few buyers of his paintings and found it difficult to support his family.

He and Amelie had two sons and a daughter. Amelie Matisse set up a hat shop in Paris to earn income for the family. She continued to serve frequently as a model for her husband.

Begins romance with color

In 1906 Matisse traveled to Italy and North Africa, both of which strongly influenced his style. In Italy he admired the frescoes of the pre-Renaissance Italian artist Giotto, with their simple, monumental style. In North Africa he was drawn to the brilliant colors and decorative patterns of Islamic art. He brought back from this trip pottery, cloths, carpets, and other

Harmony in Red, 1908. Approx. 71" x 97". State Hermitage Museum, Leningrad. © 1995 Succession H. Matisse, Paris/Artists Rights Society (ARS), New York. Giraudon/Art Resource, NY.

items, which he often used in his paintings. His *Blue Nude (Souvenir of Biskra)* reflects these influences and his love of the human figure. Yet anatomy would ultimately take a back seat to design; in the next few years, rich colors and decorative patterns, including those of vines and flowers, seemed to over-run his paintings; in *Harmony in Red,* the pattern of the wall-paper and tablecloth leave little space in the painting for the woman standing at the table.

Matisse is also notable for repeating parts of previous paint-ings in newer works. For instance, in a **still life** from 1909, the viewer can see a section of his earlier painting *La Danse. La Danse,* along with a companion painting, *La Musique,* was com-missioned by a Russian businessman named Sergei Shchukin, a great supporter of Matisse in these years. Matisse visited him in Moscow several times, and Shchukin eventually owned 37 of his paintings. In 1923 Shchukin and another Russian collector opened the first museum of contemporary Western art in Mos-cow, including 48 of Matisse's works.

Matisse also used the freedom of fauvism in his early sculp-tures. He worked with sculpture throughout his career, adapting for the medium his many concepts of form and space.

Around 1910 Matisse's style underwent another trans-formation. He delved into approaches derived from **cubism** and began using subtler colors, more simplified figures, and a greater number of geometric shapes. Matisse was never a cub-ist, but as with impressionism, he was able to incorporate many of the school's ideas and theories into his own style. This is evident in his 1911 painting *The Painter's Family,* in which the space is divided into multiple rectangular areas covered with decorative patterns of wallpaper, oriental rug designs, and upholstery prints.

After World War I Matisse began spending a substantial portion of each year in the south of France and eventually settled there permanently. Under the influence of the south's warm, sunny weather, his colors brightened again, and pat-terns and decorations became more prominent. He wrote that after many years of exploration, his art finally "had established

a new clarity and simplicity of its own." Toward the end of the 1920s, Matisse took a trip around the world, spending six months in Tahiti, where Frenchman **Paul Gauguin** (see entry) had done so much of his painting, and also traveling to the United States.

Soon after this visit, he received a commission from the Barnes Foundation in Pennsylvania to paint a **mural** in their museum, which contained many impressionist and post-impressionist works. This was the first of several interior design commissions Matisse accepted in the ensuing years. The largest project, often considered the masterpiece of his career, was the design of a chapel in the French town of Vence. Matisse created the stained-glass windows, interior decor, devotional objects, and clothing for the clergy. The chapel was dedicated in 1951.

Who Were Les Fauves?

At the 1905 Salon exhibition in Paris, the paintings of Henri Matisse, Andre Derain, Maurice de Vlaminck, and others were hung together on the walls of one exhibit room. In the center of the room was a very traditional marble sculpture of a nude woman. "Donatello parmi les fauves!"—"Donatello among the wild beasts!"—cried one art critic as he viewed the wildly colored paintings. The Renaissance artist Donatello, known for the beauty of his sculptures, may well have been as shocked as the Parisians of 1905 by the style that came to be called fauvism.

While the fauvist style was surprising at the time, its lineage can be traced through several earlier trends. Matisse and his colleagues were greatly stimulated by several large exhibits in Paris between 1901 and 1905 that featured the works of Paul Cézanne, Paul Gauguin, and Vincent van Gogh. These painters' treatment of space and color was especially interesting to the younger artists of the day. Many were experimenting with simplifying form and using color in a variety of ways. The impressionists and their followers had begun these explorations into color and light roughly 40 years earlier.

Matisse and several contemporaries had an extraordinary experience in the summer of 1905 while painting in the south of France. The rampant sunlight and lush colors of the Mediterranean climate seemed to liberate them completely from their traditional painting styles. They began to employ color freely, without regard for the constraints of **realism**. Color alone, they began to believe, could give structure to a painting. They no longer felt bound to the careful modeling and use of **perspective** they had learned in art school. Through the placement of complementary colors—red and green or blue and orange, for example—they found it possible to make certain elements jump out at the viewer or conversely, recede into space. Works that at first glance seem wild and random come into focus as powerfully emotional renderings, thanks to a painstakingly strategic use of paint. With color as their chief element, these artists could suggest space, generate light, and capture emotion. This revolutionary development marked the birth of fauvism.

Fauvist art became renowned for its pure colors: vivid greens, deep blues, bright reds, and sunny yellows. Using quick, direct brush strokes, the painters conveyed an energy and freedom that was totally new in its day. No wonder Parisian viewers were startled: they were accustomed to restrained and "proper" art. The "wild beasts," their work nearly bursting from the canvas, caused quite an uproar—and brought fine art to a new level.

Cuts out

During the 1930s Matisse turned to designing and illustrating books. He began working with geometric and abstract shapes cut out of colored paper, silhouetting these against multihued backgrounds. Matisse's most famous book, *Jazz,* dates from 1947. The vivid colors, flowing shapes, and rhythmic feel evoke the qualities of that musical form. Matisse's works were exhibited often during the 1930s in major cities across Europe and the United States. At a large exhibition in Paris in 1936, an entire room was devoted to his paintings.

In the 1940s and 1950s Matisse became increasingly handicapped due to illness. During the World War II years, he was often confined to his bed. His works from this period are smaller and include numerous book illustrations. These creations have a pronounced serenity about them, all the more remarkable since both Matisse's wife and daughter were arrested by the Nazis during this time. Amelie Matisse suffered two three-month prison sentences, and Marguerite Matisse was placed in solitary confinement, charged with resistance activities.

War's end saw an increase in Matisse's activity. He often worked from a wheelchair or in bed, sketching designs on the wall with a piece of charcoal attached to a long pole. His last paintings recalled his favorite themes of female figures and interiors and include *Large Red Interior* from 1948. He spent many hours directing his assistants to find the perfect arrangements of his paper cutouts. Matisse passed the last years of his life designing the chapel at Vence and working on his cutouts. These free-form shapes brought together all of Matisse's ideas, from painting, sculpture, and the decorative arts. Despite his infirmities, he continued working until his death at the age of 84, a maverick to the end.

Masterworks

1905	*Woman with the Hat*
1906	*Blue Nude (Souvenir of Biskra)*
1908	*Harmony in Red*
1911	*The Painter's Family*
1925	*Decorative Figure on an Ornamental Background*
1928	*Odalisques*
1935	*Pink Nude*
1946	*Polynesia, the Sea*
1948	*Large Red Interior*

Michelangelo

Born March 6, 1475
Caprese, Italy
Died February 18, 1564
Rome, Italy

"The best of artists has no concept / Not already held within the shell / Of a stone block. He reaches it / Only when his hand follows the guidance of his mind and soul."

Michelangelo was one of the great geniuses of the Italian Renaissance. He has been called the finest sculptor and draftsman of all time, ranks among the most gifted painters and architects in history, and was also a skilled poet. Although his life was not particularly happy, the body of work he left posterity displays an extraordinary beauty and spiritual grandeur. Since Michelangelo's time, virtually every artist worthy of that title has studied the creations of this master.

Michelangelo Buonarroti was born in a small town near Florence, Italy. His father, Lodovico Buonarroti Simoni, was a mild-mannered man who held a variety of low-level government jobs, none of them for very long. Francesca Miniato del Sera, the artist's mother, was quite young and in fragile health at the time of his birth; she died when he was only six, leaving him and four brothers in their father's care. Michelangelo was sent away to live with a stonecutter's family in the mountains. Many years later, he allegedly said that his love of stone came directly from the milk of the stonecutter's wife, who had nursed him when he was an infant.

Michelangelo began school when he was seven but often sneaked away to draw. Florence was filled with paintings and sculptures by great artists like the fourteenth-century painter, sculptor, and architect Giotto, early fifteenth-century painter Masaccio, and Florentine sculptors Donatello and Ghiberti. Michelangelo studied them all. His father insisted that the boy stay in school and become a government bureaucrat, but Michelangelo's determination finally won him over. At the age of 13 his father apprenticed him to the painting workshop of two well-respected artists in Florence, the Ghirlandaio brothers. Being an apprentice meant that Michelangelo would learn a trade by assisting the artists, performing whatever tasks were assigned him; his only compensation was the opportunity to study their techniques, which included painting and **fresco,** the art of painting on freshly spread moist plaster with water-based pigments. The Ghirlandaios immediately recognized the boy's developing talent. After two years he realized he had learned all he could from them and left their workshop.

Nourished by cultural activity in Florence

Michelangelo's natural abilities and education were supplemented by the nourishing environment of Florence, which was then the cultural center of Europe. Artists, writers, scientists, and philosophers gathered there, and there was widespread interest in all forms of education and the arts. This period, from about 1300 to 1650, was called the **Renaissance,** and Michelangelo, along with his fellow artists **Leonardo da Vinci** (see entry) and Raphael, are considered to represent the height of this flowering. Many noble families and merchants of the era became patrons of the arts, providing money and sometimes lodging in exchange for the creation of artworks, which often glorified the patron. Two of the most important groups of patrons were the Medici family of Florence and the several popes who headed the Roman Catholic Church during that time. Both played crucial roles in Michelangelo's life.

◀ *Portrait* (p. 296): Michelangelo, *by Daniel de Volterra. Reproduced by permission of The Bettmann Archive.*

Michelangelo ultimately chose to become a sculptor, and at the age of 16 he went to study at a new school sponsored by the most powerful man in Florence, Lorenzo de Medici. This mentor also detected a special talent in Michelangelo and treated him like a son. Michelangelo was allowed to attend de Medici's gatherings and meet the most famous artists, poets, and thinkers of the age. It was at one of these functions that Michelangelo got into a fight with another student, who punched him in the nose. For the rest of his life, Michelangelo had a flattened nose, which makes him easily recognizable in portraits.

In 1492 de Medici died; this forced the young artist to begin his professional career in earnest. During the next few years Michelangelo was enabled by the director of a local hospital to study the anatomy of corpses awaiting burial. The careful study of bones, muscles, and organs gave him an unusual understanding of the structure of the human body. He was able to transfer this to his work as few other artists have, and for the rest of his career, Michelangelo painted and sculpted little else besides human figures.

Creates sensation with *Pietà* and *David*

As a sculptor, Michelangelo required wealthy patrons to pay for the expensive marble he used. Besides the Medicis, the richest patron of the era was the pope. In 1497 Michelangelo was summoned to Rome to create a statue for a chapel at the Basilica of St. Peter. When the statue was finished and displayed in 1499, few believed that an artist of only 23 years could have sculpted such a masterpiece. The work, called the *Pietà*, is a traditional religious scene of the Virgin Mary holding the body of Jesus after his crucifixion. Much of the power of this piece—and of the artist's other sculptures—derives from its extremely lifelike textures; the cloth of Mary's dress, though made of marble, appears soft and flowing; the skin of the two figures seems warm and supple. Viewers often try to touch Michelangelo's statues to see if they are really made of stone.

Pietà, 1498-99. Marble, 5'9". St. Peter's, Vatican, Rome. ▶
Reproduced by permission of Alinari/Art Resource, NY.

What Do We Mean by the "Renaissance"?

The Renaissance—literally "rebirth"—is a term historians have used to describe a period of tremendous cultural ambition and achievement in Western Europe. Much of this development resulted from the partial secularization, or slight movement away from religious doctrine, in the culture (though some scholars disagree with the traditional view that the Renaissance simply "happened" at some discernible time "after" the Middle Ages). Attitudes toward learning and aesthetics, theories concerning the nature of beauty, changed. In the several centuries preceding the Renaissance, almost all education and art in Europe was controlled by the Church, which dictated that art's purpose was the glorification of God and religion—and frequently the Church itself and its leaders. Around 1400 the cultural climate began to change, due in part to the presence of new economic powers outside the Church with their own artistic agendas. Such developments helped spark a revival—or renaissance—of interest in classical Greek and Roman literature and art. The partial secularization occasioned by this revival sparked a revolution in science, mathematics, literature, and the arts.

Florence, Italy, had become the center of the Renaissance by about 1450. Throughout what is now Italy, a growing class of wealthy merchants and noble families found themselves with sufficient leisure to explore new areas of learning, as well as the necessary funds to sponsor artists and scientists. Previously, a wealthy family may have commissioned a work for their local church and asked the artist to include the family in the painting of their patron saint or some other religious depiction. During the Renaissance, nobles wanted impressive images of themselves to hang in their villas

When word of the *Pietà* reached Florence, Michelangelo was invited to execute a statue for the city; on his return, he received a tremendous block of marble with which several other sculptors had grappled unsuccessfully. Compelled by this shapeless stone mass, the sculptor declared his intention to free the figure within it. What he released from the marble is probably his most renowned sculpture: the 14-foot-high figure of the young biblical figure David preparing to fight the giant Goliath. The beauty, dignity, and strength of this *David* have moved people for almost 500 years.

or castles. Portraiture became a new way for artists to earn a living.

Many Renaissance artists studied a wide variety of disciplines: painting, sculpture, anatomy, mathematics, science. They looked to these structured pursuits to help them find the harmony and balance they believed existed in nature. It is from these figures that the term "Renaissance Man"—meaning someone who excels in diverse fields—later passed into general usage. Much of the creative work of the period that traditional historians have labeled the Early Renaissance involved the quest for rational, orderly principles by which natural harmony could be realized. It is frequently argued that the masters of the so-called High Renaissance went beyond these rules, that their individual genius and creativity resulted in works that exceeded the constraints of reason and achieved a universal power.

The High Renaissance lasted only about 25 years, from roughly 1495 to 1520. The artists working then remain the most celebrated of Western art. They include the painter, sculptor, architect, engineer, and scientist Leonardo da Vinci; sculptor and painter Michelangelo; painters Raphael, **Titian** (see entry), and Giorgone; and the architect Donato Bramante. These figures helped forge a new role for artists in society: for the first time, an artist's signature was closely associated with his work and valued by collectors; buyers sought out the works of specific creators.

Social circumstances, economic prosperity, and more liberal attitudes toward education and religion all contributed to the European cultural blossoming historians have traditionally dubbed the Renaissance. For centuries it has been regarded as a pinnacle of human creativity and aspiration.

Reluctantly paints Sistine Chapel

Shortly thereafter, Pope Julius II—who, contemplating his mortality, was planning an impressive mausoleum for his burial—sent for Michelangelo and commissioned him to sculpt 40 statues for the tomb. The artist immediately set out for the mountains where the marble was cut; he spent eight months choosing each block. Michelangelo enjoyed living with the marble cutters and overseeing their work. On his return to Rome, however, he learned that the pope had changed his mind and

instead wanted Michelangelo to paint the ceiling of the large Sistine Chapel, one of the papal palaces. Michelangelo was furious; he told the pope he was a sculptor, not a painter, and certainly not an expert in the technique of fresco, which was required for the plaster ceiling. He fled Rome, but Pope Julius insisted he return. For four years Michelangelo slaved on his back under the huge ceiling, over 60 feet in the air and roughly the size of two and a half tennis courts. He experimented with various fresco methods and dismissed his assistants, working alone for part of the project.

The results were extraordinary. The Sistine Chapel ceiling is considered one of the wonders of the world; it features over 300 figures illustrating biblical scenes such as the creation of the heavens and the earth and the stories of Adam and Eve and Noah, among many others. Today's visitors to the chapel have been fortunate to see Michelangelo's epic in a form resembling its original state: specialists spent nearly the entire 1980s meticulously cleaning centuries of dirt from the frescos. Even these experts were stunned as they slowly uncovered the vibrancy of Michelangelo's colors. His fresco technique, about which he had initially had misgivings, was adequate to sustain his work for four centuries.

Michelangelo was only about 37 years old when he finally finished the Sistine ceiling. He spent 50 more years creating unique and beautiful works for various patrons, including other popes and members of the Medici family. He returned to the Sistine Chapel roughly a quarter century later to paint a scene of the Last Judgment—the biblical narrative of the world's end—on a wall. He fashioned numerous sculptures for the tombs of Lorenzo de Medici's son and nephew. And as an architect, he designed the dome of St. Peter's Basilica. When Florence feared a military attack, it enlisted Michelangelo to build fortifications for the city.

Despite his many gifts and considerable fame, Michelangelo lived a life of isolation and, to some degree, dissatisfaction. He spent many years on works that were not of his choosing, yet he attacked each project with profound intensity. He was nearly 90 when he died—an extremely advanced age for his era—and continued sculpting to the end.

Michelangelo's towering stature derives, in part, from his ability to invest the human figures he limned in stone and on canvas with a luminous energy. His adoration of the human form allowed him to give a soulful individuality to the mythological and biblical figures he portrayed, a distinctly human character that carries an ageless appeal. His work ranks among the finest examples of what is still considered the Golden Age of art in the Western world.

Masterworks

Sculpture

1498-99	*Pietà*
1501-04	*David*
1506-13	*Moses*
1513	*Dying Captive*
1526-31	*Night/Day, Dawn/Evening*
1547	*Florence Pietà*
1555-64	*Rondanini Pietà*

Painting/fresco

1503-04	*Holy Family with St. John (Doni Tondo)*
1508-12	Sistine Chapel ceiling
1536-41	*Last Judgment,* Sistine Chapel

Architecture

1547-1564	Dome of St. Peter's Basilica, Rome

Piet Mondrian

Born March 7, 1872
Maersfoort, Netherlands
Died February 1, 1944
New York, New York

"Like religion, art is superhuman and cultivates the superhuman element in man, and it is consequently a means of human evolution."

Until he was almost 40 years old, Piet Mondrian was known primarily as a competent painter of landscapes and other traditional subjects in his native Holland. When he became aware of the ideas of modern art, however, Mondrian adopted them completely and pushed them forward as few other artists had. By the end of his life he was considered one of the world's most important abstract painters, having jettisoned representation altogether in favor of compositions comprised exclusively of geometric shapes and color. Motivated by a desire to simplify art to its very essence, Mondrian substantially influenced modern art in both its theory and practice and held significant sway over contemporary architecture and fashion as well.

Mondrian, born Pieter Mondriaan, was one of five children of a middle-class family from a small Dutch town. His father, also named Pieter Mondriaan, was a schoolmaster and enjoyed drawing as a hobby. Other family members were also artists; young Pieter had his first painting lessons from an uncle.

The family lived by very strict religious principles enforced by the dominating Pieter senior, who insisted that his son also become a teacher. The boy decided that he wanted to teach drawing and, after studying hard in local schools, convinced his father to let him go to the Academy of Fine Arts in the capital city of Amsterdam.

Avoids Amsterdam nightlife while in art school

Mondrian was 20 years old when he arrived in the city. He studied diligently for three years at the academy and—unlike his peers—avoided Amsterdam's world-renowned nightlife. He then attended drawing classes at night and held a variety of jobs to support himself, including illustrating science textbooks, teaching art, and copying paintings in museums.

Mondrian was a capable, if traditional, painter; he displayed a marked preference in this phase of his artistic development for landscape scenes of rural Holland, with its windmills, churches, and wide, flat plains. He also painted flowers, often devoting an entire canvas to one meticulously observed blossom. Until about 1908 Mondrian had little exposure to the experiments percolating in the art world.

In the summer of 1908 Mondrian spent time with a group of painters on a small island in Holland. Among them were two older Dutch artists who strongly influenced Mondrian, Jan Sluyters and Jan Toorop. Both of these men had been to Paris and greatly admired the work of **Henri Matisse,** their countryman **Vincent van Gogh** (see entries), and other exponents of the style called **fauvism**. Through Sluyters and Toorop, Mondrian learned about radical new forms; he immediately began to expand his technical horizons. His colors became more intense and were applied more randomly, and he explored different kinds of brush strokes. His most famous painting from this time, *The Red Tree,* depicts a large, leafless tree, the trunk and branches of which he rendered in reds and purples against a bright blue background so that it would bristle with energy. One can discern the evolution of Mondrian's style during this period by comparing his many tree paintings.

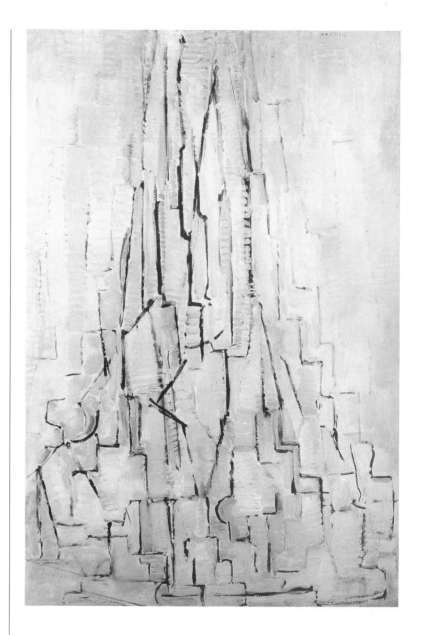

Composition refined to its bare bones

In 1911 Mondrian went to Paris and quickly became caught up in the excitement created by the new artistic style known as **cubism.** The strong geometric lines of this mode greatly appealed to Mondrian; he appropriated a number of cubist ideas and spent his years in Paris hammering out a unique style of his own. He simplified forms, condensed shapes, and removed details, all in pursuit of composition refined to its bare bones.

Mondrian immersed himself in the various theories and philosophies of art throughout his life; one writer commented that he painted merely to illustrate such ideas. Yet Mondrian's theoretical bent hasn't prevented viewers from perceiving great beauty in his work. The pinnacle of his explorations came when he eliminated all subjects from his paintings, making them completely **abstract.** His most prominent works contain only vertical and horizontal lines—usually black—and are limited in hue to the primary colors—red, blue, and yellow. Mondrian's style, which he called "plasticism," remains instantly recognizable.

Mondrian detailed his many artistic philosophies in a magazine called *De Stijl,* which he founded with fellow artist Theo Van Doesburg in 1917. De Stijl was also the name given to the style they developed; it stressed exactness, abstraction, and strict adherence to the formal theories Mondrian and others held. Members of the De Stijl school were not only painters but also architects, designers, and interior decorators. Most eventually broke with the group to embrace other styles, but De Stijl remained a powerful influence on twentieth-century design.

Work exhibited in Europe and the United States

Throughout the 1920s and 1930s, Mondrian worked to more fully delineate his ideas, and his paintings appeared in exhibitions in Paris, New York, and elsewhere. In 1938 he moved to London, anticipating that war would soon begin in Europe, but he was forced to leave the city less than two years later when German air raids there began to make life very difficult. He went to New York in October 1940.

The modern, urban environment of New York City entranced Mondrian; he loved the geometry of the buildings and their lighted windows at night, the horizontals and verticals of the streets, and the tall skyscrapers reaching for the sky. Mondrian's last compositions, painted in New York, are among his most popular. Gone are the heavy black grid lines. The

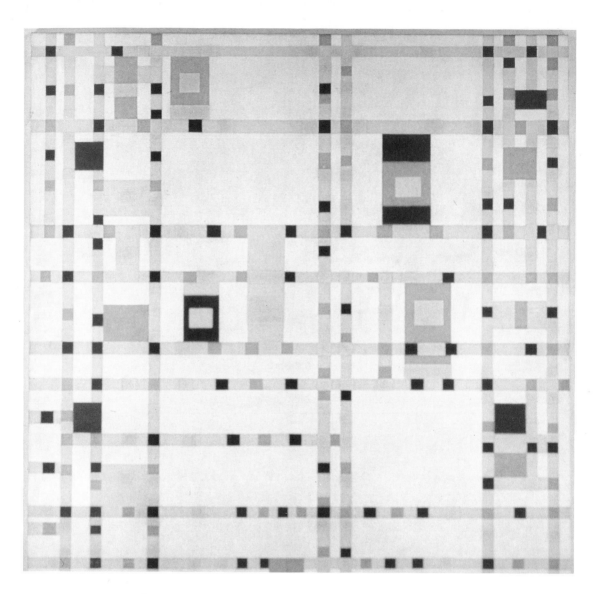

arrangements of yellow, black, and red squares hum with the energy of city blocks and the pulsing rhythms of jazz, which inspired many a painter of the era. For more than 20 years, Mondrian had given no descriptive titles to his paintings; they were called simply *Composition No. 1* or *Composition with Red, Blue, and Yellow.* In New York—apparently intoxicated by city life and American music—he gave his last works titles like *Broadway Boogie-Woogie* and *Victory Boogie-Woogie.*

But Mondrian lived little more than three years in New York; he died of pneumonia in 1944 at the age of 72. Although he had led a generally quiet and solitary life, he helped to pioneer a style through which he vividly expressed a shared vision of modern life. His influence has been wide indeed, from the work of kinetic artist **Alexander Calder** (see entry) to the avant-garde fashion designers of the 1960s.

Masterworks

1900	*Mill by the Water*
1909	*The Red Tree*
1912	*Still Life with Ginger Pot*
1915	*Pier and Ocean*
1917	*Composition in Blue B*
	Composition with Red, Blue, and Yellow
1942	*Broadway Boogie-Woogie*
1943	*Victory Boogie-Woogie*

Claude Monet

Born November 14, 1840
Paris, France

Died December 5, 1926
Giverny, France

"Above all, I wanted to be true and exact. A landscape, for me, does not exist at all as such, because the aspect changes at every moment, but it lives through its surroundings by the light and air, which vary continually."

The shimmering light and breathtaking colors of Claude Monet's work have made him one of the world's most popular artists for almost a century. His studies of the changing effects of sunlight on haystacks, churches, fields, and water gardens were unique in his time and extremely influential to subsequent generations. As a founder of the style known as **impressionism**, Monet broke with many traditions to create a new method of painting—and of seeing the world around us. Without his innovations, the course of twentieth-century art would have been quite different.

Claude-Oscar Monet was born in Paris. When he was five years old, his family moved to Le Havre, a port on the Atlantic Ocean northeast of Paris. Monet's father owned a grocery store from which he supplied sailors and shipping companies. Young Monet most likely encountered many colorful characters in his father's store. He became known for his talent at drawing caricatures of people around town. In fact, he was not particularly successful at school because he spent most of his time drawing. When he was a teenager, he began to earn money for his portraiture. He met his first important teacher, Eugène Boudin, when some of his drawings were exhibited next to Boudin's paintings in the window of a local shop.

◀ *Portrait (p. 310):*
Photograph by
Paul Nadar.

Began painting out-of-doors

Monet was not a fan of Boudin's work, but Boudin convinced him to join him in painting out-of-doors, instead of in a studio—an unusual practice at the time. Monet loved painting in the open air and did so for the rest of his life. He was able to do so early in his career because paint had begun to become available in tubes that artists could carry with them. Before, they were forced to mix colored powder and oil in jars, a very messy process that was particularly clumsy outside the studio.

Monet's family was not keen on his chosen profession; they wanted him to join the family grocery business. But when he was 19, one of his aunts who loved to paint gave him the money to go to Paris to study art. Still, Monet was not satisfied with the traditional styles that were being taught there. He longed to get outdoors and paint the sunlight and trees and water. In Paris Monet met other young painters who shared his desires, **Pierre-Auguste Renoir, Edouard Manet** (see entries), Alfred Sisley, and Frédéric Bazille among them. Monet's family continued to scorn his career choice and the artist was frequently forced to borrow money from friends.

In 1866 one of Monet's paintings, a large portrait of a young woman in a green dress, was accepted into the traditional **Salon** exhibit sponsored by the French Ministry of Art. This success convinced his family that he was on the right track after all, and they began funding him again—until they found out that he was living with the young woman in the painting, Camille Doncieux. They ordered him to return home and cut him off financially. Meanwhile, Doncieux gave birth to Monet's first child, a son they named Jean. Monet began regular travel between Paris and the north of France in an effort to earn money to support his new family; he borrowed from anyone he could. It was a difficult

| Claude Monet

Impression: Sunrise, *1872.*
Marmottan Museum, Paris.
Reproduced by permission
of Scala/Art Resource, NY.

time, but he nonetheless managed to paint many pictures. In 1870 he married Doncieux and the couple went to London to escape the war raging between France and Prussia.

The birth of impressionism

After the war Monet and his family settled in Argenteuil, a small town near Paris. He put together a floating studio of sorts and painted scenes on the river there. Other painters visited Argenteuil to paint with Monet. He was able to make a small living because an art dealer in Paris believed in the new style promoted by Monet and his friends Renoir, Camille Pissarro, and **Paul Cézanne** (see entry). They organized an exhibit of their work in Paris in 1874. One of the paintings Monet contributed to the show was titled *Impression: Sunrise*. Neither critics nor the public took the work of these young painters seriously. One newspaper writer derisively referred to them as "impressionists." Monet and his colleagues wore the term like a badge of honor. Ultimately, the style called "impressionism" became the most important movement of nineteenth-century art.

The traditional subjects of the day in the visual arts were figures and events from history, religious narratives, or classical mythology. The predominant style featured dark, muted colors and clear, sharply outlined forms. Monet and the other impressionists, considered radical in their methods, longed to capture the ordinary sights that comprised their lives. They attempted to approximate the "impression" of light shining on water, or of water splashing on rocks. They experimented with pigment, trying to achieve just the right combination of hue and light to illustrate what their eyes took in out-of-doors. In Monet's work, the character of brush strokes was very important. If the viewer stands very close to one of his paintings, it is difficult to make out the subject—the image before the viewer appears merely as dabs and slashes of paint. But when the viewer steps back, the colorful brush strokes combine to form people strolling down a street or flowers in a field.

Despite the withering criticism he received, Monet continued to paint in the impressionist style. And he began to find a few bold souls who expressed an interest in the results. One of them was Ernest Hochedé, who owned some large department stores in Paris. He bought several of Monet's paintings. The Hochedé family, including Ernest and Alice and their six children, became friendly with the Monet family. But in 1877 many of Hochedé's department stores failed and he was forced to leave France. Alice Hochedé and her children remained behind. That summer she and the Monet family rented a summer house together in a small town. Soon thereafter, Monet's second son, Michel, was born. There were eight children in the house and very little money. Then, Madame Monet developed tuberculosis; she died that fall. Monet was devastated and found it almost impossible to paint. Alice Hochedé labored to care for him and all of the children. They stayed in the summer house for several years because they could not afford to return to Paris.

Claude Monet

Impressionism:
Exploring How the Eye Sees

The artistic style most prevalent in nineteenth-century Paris was characterized by a traditional romanticism, subjects generally taken from history, religious narratives, or classical mythology. Painters employed subtle, somber colors and well-defined forms. The stroke of the brush was in no way evident. Such works were shown each year at a large exhibition known as the **Salon.** Paintings in the Salon were selected by judges who were themselves chosen by the government-run Ecole des Beaux Arts (School of Fine Arts). It was crucial to an artist's success that his work appear at the Salon.

Thus there was great outrage in 1874 when a group of young painters held their own exhibit of vividly colored paintings full of wild, choppy brush strokes. These works depicted scenes considered improper for painting, among them ordinary folk strolling down city streets, young women in their seats at the theater, and a girl and her mother playing hide-and-seek in a field. The exhibition met with much negative criticism and ridicule. Critics considered the paintings crude and unfinished. Viewers complained that the artists had only provided an "impression" of their subjects. One writer mocked the painters by calling them "impressionists," after a painting in the show titled *Impression: Sunrise*. That canvas was the work of Claude Monet. Monet and his colleagues Pierre-Auguste Renoir, Paul Cézanne, Alfred Sisley, Camille Pissarro, Berthe Morisot, and Edgar Degas took this insult and turned it to their advantage; they called their new style "impressionism."

Though these innovative painters actually worked in a variety of modes, they were lumped together because they rejected the official art of the Salons and the established foundation of painting, whereby scenes are arranged with models in a studio. They began to paint out-of-doors, trying to capture exactly how their eye perceived their surroundings. These rebels were concerned with the everyday life of the present, not the perfected scenes of ancient history that were approved by the Salon. They longed to suggest the re-

Eventually, Monet began to paint again. During the 1870s and early 1880s he participated in several shows with the other impressionist painters. His work of this period was dominated by landscapes and seascapes, among them *The Cliff Walk at Pourville* and *The Cliff at Etretat,* which depicts a large rock formation jutting out into the sea. He also painted the swirling

flection of light on a particular setting, as well as represent the particular quality of that light. The group of friends spent many hours together in cafés and studios discussing how to achieve the goal of painting nature. Their exchange of ideas brought about the revolution of impressionism.

The styles the impressionists developed over the course of the 1870s and 1880s varied according to each artist's interests and skills. There was no common set of rules, but several elements appeared throughout the movement. Contrasts of color defined the shapes and outlines of objects rather than clearly determined lines. This lent the scenes depicted an indistinct, shimmering look. Many impressionists used little or no black paint, as did most traditional painters, especially to cast shadow. The impressionists instead relied on deep shades of purple and blue to create shading, which afforded their work a unique brightness.

These painters also employed new scientific ideas about vision in their work; they realized that the human eye does not see faraway objects as clearly as those close by. Thus they did not paint objects in the distance in the same manner as those in the foreground; the *impression* of depth was all that was necessary. They also discovered that the eye will naturally combine bits of color when viewed from a distance. Indeed, when a viewer looks closely at an impressionist painting, he or she will detect only choppy splashes of colored paint. But when the viewer steps back, the melange of colored brush strokes meld together to become figures walking in the distance, flowers in a garden, or boats on a lake.

The impressionists mounted several exhibitions during the 1870s and 1880s. Painters working in other styles joined their group, many of them going on to found entirely new schools of painting, including **pointillism, fauvism,** and several post-impressionist styles. In fact, most of the styles that have developed in twentieth-century art can be traced to the new ideas about color and light that the impressionists spearheaded. In addition to its importance as a step toward the birth of what is now considered modern art, the work of Monet and his fellow painters, with its often peaceful imagery and eye-pleasing colors, is among the best loved in all the world.

steam and smoke of a steam engine at a station in Gare Saint-Lazare. Another famous painting of this time is *Rue Montorgueil Decked Out with Flags,* a Parisian street scene in which every window and doorway is draped with the French flag in celebration of a national holiday. The colorful banners, which seem to wave in the wind, lend the work great energy and excitement.

Haystack. Reproduced by permission of The Bettmann Archive.

Settled near scenic Giverny

As soon as Monet was able to sell a few paintings, he began to look for a more suitable home for himself, Madame Hochedé, and the eight children. He located the perfect residence in the small town of Giverny, roughly 60 miles from Paris. Monet lived in this house from 1883 until his death in 1926—over 40 years. He spent much time planting the garden there, which grew both flowers and vegetables. The children were charged with weeding and watering. There was also a river nearby where the children could swim and boat. The garden and river provided inspiration for many of Monet's paintings. The house and gardens are today the Monet Museum. They are maintained very much as they were when Monet and his extended family lived there.

In 1892, after receiving word that Ernest Hochedé had died, Monet and Alice Hochedé were married. By then Monet's paintings had become not only accepted, but highly prized; though he hated to part with them, the works earned him a handsome sum when he did. Art dealers from as far away as America journeyed to Giverny to see Monet. It was during this time that he began to paint his acclaimed series. Focusing on a single subject, he would paint it at various times of the day to demonstrate how the shifting light changed the appearance of the scene. Day after day, he would return to the same spot to capture just the light he sought. He painted haystacks, poplar trees, the cathedral of the city of Rouen, and the bridge over the river near his home. Perhaps his most famous series was produced near the end of his life. He had created a water garden at his home at Giverny and painted large canvases of the water lilies growing there. He painted them almost exclusively for the last ten years of his life. The results are on display in an impressionist art museum in Paris; just two of them take up the wall space of an entire room.

As he grew older, Monet suffered from cataracts, a painful eye disease that rendered him almost blind. He continued to paint, but many of his pictures took on a predominantly reddish hue and appeared blurry. When he finally underwent surgery to correct the condition, the vivid colors and sun-dappled forms that had made him famous returned to his paintings. By the 1920s Monet was arguably the best-known artist in France—if not in all the world. Honors and praises were heaped on him, though he did not pay them much mind. He was never quite satisfied that he could capture light and color exactly as he saw it. But admirers of his art concur that what he did capture was extraordinary. Indeed, a *New York Times* contributor attested shortly after Monet's death that the artist "lifted landscape painting into a region of shimmering illusion that ... had a singularly enlivening effect upon the spirits—as when the sun itself comes out and clears away the fog and darkness."

Masterworks

1866	*Women in the Garden*
	Terrace at the Seaside, Sainte-Adresse
1872	*Impression: Sunrise*
1874	*Wild Poppies*
1877	*Gare Saint-Lazare*
1878	*Rue Montorgueil Decked Out with Flags*
1882	*The Cliff Walk*
1887	*Boating on the River Epte*
1891	*Poplars*
	Haystacks
1894	*Cathedral at Rouen*
1899-1900	*Water Garden at Giverny*
1903	*The Houses of Parliament*
1916-23	*Water Lilies*

Henry Moore

Born July 30, 1898
Castleford, Yorkshire, England
Died August 31, 1986
Much Hadham, Hertfordshire, England

"All good art contains abstract and surreal elements together, just as it contains classical as well as romantic elements: order and surprise, intellect and imagination, conscious and unconscious."

Henry Moore was one of the most popular and most groundbreaking sculptors of the twentieth century. From the 1960s on, for many a new museum, bank, theater, hotel, or corporate building seeking an impressive onsite sculpture, a Moore work served to bestow elegance and sophistication. Best known for large stone reclining figures, as well as depictions of mothers with children, Moore was fascinated by the art of African and pre-Columbian (before the time of Christopher Columbus) cultures. He forged his distinctive style by combining Western approaches with these ancient traditions; this hybrid resulted in works that abound with life, beauty, and imagination.

Henry Moore grew up in a small coal-mining town in northern England. His father, Raymond Spencer Moore, was a miner who educated himself and eventually rose to a manager's position in the mine. Mary Baker Moore, Henry's mother, was a woman of great strength and determination: during her husband's many long periods of unemployment—once he was out of work for two years—she worked as a housekeeper for a local family. This was in addition to raising Henry and his seven brothers and sisters.

Becomes entranced by work of Michelangelo

Henry Moore recalled his childhood as a happy one. His family was close and, though not wealthy, never lacked food or shelter. Moore remembered playing games with neighborhood friends and going on summer exploring expeditions in the countryside. Moore's parents insisted that their children get an education; in addition to grammar school, they attended church school on Sundays. It was the latter that first inspired thoughts of sculpture in young Henry. The head of the school often gave talks on a variety of subjects. One day he narrated the life of **Michelangelo** (see entry), whom he called "the greatest sculptor that ever lived." This phrase stuck with Moore and fueled a profound interest in Michelangelo and in art in general.

After grammar school Moore won a scholarship to attend a local secondary school. The headmaster there was very progressive and concerned with the arts. He encouraged the students to stage plays and history pageants and brought in speakers and musicians from outside the school. The art teacher also encouraged Moore, often asking his help in designing costumes and props for plays and in drawing covers for play programs; she also organized pottery and weaving classes after school hours. This teacher encouraged Moore to apply for a scholarship to a local art college, which could lead to entry into the Royal College of Art in London. Moore's father, however, did not like this idea; he wanted Henry to become a teacher like his older brothers and sisters.

The outbreak of World War I changed Moore's plans. He was 16 when the war began and had two years of secondary school remaining. He was able to complete his schooling and briefly continue his education as a student teacher. But on turning 18, he enlisted in the army, and in the summer of 1917 he was sent to the western front in France. Later that year Moore's

battalion was shelled by the Germans; some of the shells contained nerve gas. Moore and several others were sent back to London to recover from the effects.

After the war Moore took advantage of a scholarship program for veterans and enrolled in the Leeds College of Art. At the end of his second year, he passed the sculpture examination and won a scholarship to study at the Royal College of Art. After what seemed like an endless climb, his career was finally beginning.

Discovers pre-Columbian art

Moore spent three years at the Royal College of Art: two to earn his diploma and an extra year in advanced studies. The institution's location afforded him the opportunity to visit London's wealth of museums, which offered a curriculum as important as his formal studies. He spent considerable time at the British Museum, where he discovered compelling sculpture collections from Africa, Polynesia, and the pre-Columbian Americas. These exerted a tremendous influence on Moore's development. In Paris in 1925 he saw a plaster cast of a sculpture of the Mayan rain god Chac Mool. It summarized for him the elements he most admired in non-Western art. He later wrote of four qualities he detected in it that he hoped to achieve in his own work: first, its "stoniness," that is, its truthfulness to the material used; second, the power and sensitivity of the image; third, variety and creativity in form; and fourth, full three-dimensional form. Moore's work throughout his career, especially his many reclining figures, can be understood through the inspiration this Mayan figure provided him.

From 1924 to 1939 Moore maintained his own studio and taught sculpture. He traveled frequently to Paris and was also spurred creatively by excursions to Italy and Spain. He exhibited his work frequently in London and countless other cosmopolitan locales; his creations were first displayed in New York City in 1936. In 1929 he married Irina Radetsky, a painting student at the Royal College of Art. They lived in several locations around London before purchasing a farmhouse in the country in 1940, where they remained for the rest of Moore's life. In 1946 their daughter was born.

As it did for all of England, World War II brought great upheaval to the sculptor's life: Moore's London studio was damaged by bombs during German shelling in 1940. Materials were impossibly scarce, and without a studio Moore could do little sculpting for almost five years. He did find work, however, as an official war artist; his assignment was to depict the reactions of the people of London as they sought protection in underground shelters from the nightly bombing by German aircraft. These were called the "Shelter Drawings"; Moore's evocative rendering of their heroism and determination in this time of crisis struck a deep chord in the British people and helped spread the artist's fame. Another important commission Moore received during the war was from a church in

Reclining Figure No. 5.
*Reproduced by permission
of Archive Photos/Express
Newspapers.*

Northhampton for a Madonna and child sculpture. The piece received high praise for its gentle dignity.

Figure of the reclining woman

After World War II Moore's reputation grew around the world; his prestige was further increased when he received first prize at a major exhibition in Venice in 1948. Throughout the 1940s and 1950s he expanded his repertoire, depicting helmeted heads, family groups, and standing figures similar to those found on native American totem poles. But his work was dominated by the figure of the reclining woman. A *New York Times* critic wrote that Moore's ideal was a statuesque, warrior-like woman, full of "endurance, protectiveness, combativity, vigilance, and heavy-limbed beauty." The large marble reclining figure he completed in 1958 for the main entrance of the UNESCO building in Paris is considered one of his greatest achievements.

During the 1950s Moore continued his travels, visiting Greece, Italy, and Mexico. In Mexico he was able to study more of the pre-Columbian art that so enchanted him, while his time in Greece prompted in him an interest in sculpted drapery. Combining the artistic stimulants from these voyages, he began producing large, bronze figures of seated women swathed in drapery. In the 1960s Moore embarked on the creation of his famous interlocking sculptures. These usually took the form of reclining figures made of two or three massive pieces of stone, which often produced the effect of a body with detached limbs. Moore's reclining figure at New York City's Lincoln Center is one of the finest examples of the series.

Moore's work was in such demand by this time that he presided over an expansive workshop and a bevy of assistants. He would make a small model (called a maquette), after completion of which assistants would be responsible for the actual carving, under his supervision.

Moore received myriad honors from his native England—including the two highest bestowed by the Queen—and honorary degrees from Oxford, Harvard, and Yale universities, among other laurels from across the globe. Though weakened by illness in the last years of his life, he continued to reside at his country home and work from a wheelchair. Since his death in 1986, Moore's work has swelled in popularity; his unprecedented fusion of Western and non-Western sculptural traditions—which became increasingly accepted as the twentieth century wore on—and honest, generous celebration of the human form has continued to delight and inspire countless artists.

Masterworks

1924-25	*Mother and Child*
1928-29	*North Wind*
1939-40	*The Helmet*
1943-44	*Madonna and Child*
1952-53	*King and Queen*
1957-58	*UNESCO Reclining Figure*
1963-65	*Reclining Figure,* Lincoln Center Sculpture
1964	*Three-Way Piece No. 2 (Archer)*
1969-70	*Reclining Figure: Arch Leg*

Isamu Noguchi

Born November 17, 1904
Los Angeles, California
Died December 30, 1988
New York, New York

"I always wanted to go beyond art objects. I wanted to reach ... a way of life, a space of life, or even a ghetto closed and defended from the world."

In his sculpture and his design of gardens and public spaces, Isamu Noguchi combined the ancient traditions of Japan with the vitality of contemporary America. Indeed, his life moved between these two very different worlds and during its course and beyond, his work has been prized by art lovers in both the East and West. Noguchi's work as a sculptor is his best known, but he also designed buildings, painted, worked in ceramics, created sets and costumes for the theater and ballet, and designed consumer products including lighting fixtures and furniture. He is remembered for bringing sculpture out of the museum and putting it in more-public places—plazas and courtyards, universities and parks.

Noguchi was the son of Yone Noguchi, a celebrated Japanese poet and art expert who spent many years in the United States. Noguchi's mother, Leonie Gilmour, was an American writer. She took her son to live in Japan when he was two years old. Realizing that he would never be completely accepted in

Japanese society because of his mixed ethnicity, she arranged for him to be educated in the United States when he was 13. He traveled alone from Japan to a small town in Indiana, where he lived with a minister's family and attended the local high school. Life there was very different from that of his childhood in Japan, and he was forced to make many adjustments.

◄ *Portrait (p. 324):
Reproduced by
permission of AP/Wide
World Photos.*

Perseveres as sculptor despite doubts

After high school Noguchi served briefly as assistant to Gutzon Borglum, the sculptor whose most famous work is the faces of four American presidents carved into Mt. Rushmore, South Dakota. Borglum examined Noguchi's artwork and declared that the young man would never be a sculptor. Profoundly discouraged, Noguchi went to New York City and began pre-medical studies at Columbia University. He didn't stay long, however, instead enrolling in sculpture classes at a local art school. His marked progress and encouragement from the school's director inspired him to definitively choose sculpture as his career. By 1927, when he was about 23, Noguchi had established a studio and shown his work at an exhibition. That year he won a fellowship award that allowed him to travel to Paris.

In Paris Noguchi worked for six months as an apprentice to the Romanian-born sculptor **Constantin Brancusi** (see entry). Brancusi was a master craftsman, greatly admired for the beautiful, highly polished finishes of his work. "Brancusi gave me respect for tools and materials," Noguchi once said. He encouraged Noguchi's love of natural media like wood and stone and introduced him to many concepts of modern art. Until then Noguchi's sculptures were traditional in style, many of them portrait busts. But the modern simplicity and **abstract** forms of Brancusi's work had a huge influence on him.

The early 1930s were filled with travel and study for Noguchi. He journeyed across Asia on the Trans-Siberian Railroad to Beijing, the capital of China. He stayed there for eight months, studying the decorative lettering of calligraphy and brush painting. He then went to Japan, where he renewed his connections to his father's family. He spent many months studying Japa-

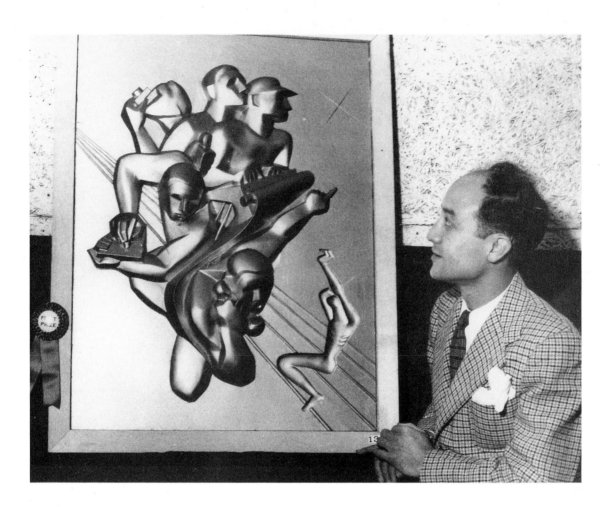

Noguchi with his award-winning model of the relief mural for the facade of the Associated Press building in Rockefeller Center in New York City, November 10, 1938. Reproduced by permission of AP/Wide World Photos.

nese ceramics and the art of Japanese gardens, especially how land can be used to create an artistic environment. It was during this period that he began to consider art as a way of addressing social ills.

Explores relationship between people and art

Noguchi unveiled his first public sculpture in Mexico City in 1935. Constructed of brick and colored cement, the work was a large relief **mural.** A relief is a sculpted shape that projects from a flat background. Working on the public wall reinforced Noguchi's belief that art should serve all people. He found that his ideas were similar to those of many prominent Mexican artists of the day, including the great mural painter **Diego Rivera** (see entry). Noguchi spent several years designing proposals for playgrounds and sculptures for community buildings and public housing. He longed to create artistic spaces for people to enjoy at work and in their neighborhoods. Few of these designs were ever realized. Noguchi did create a sculpture garden for the Ford Motor Company pavilion, however, at the 1939 New York World's Fair. He also won an important commission at that time to design a relief mural for the facade of the Associated Press building in Rockefeller Center in New York City. The huge stainless steel work eventually installed over the building's entrance weighs 10 tons.

Noguchi continued to pursue his interest in the environment and humankind's place in it. This led him to investigate the nature of leisure and how people use free space. In many of his plans for gardens and public areas, he attempted to create a space in which people could view sculpture as part of a larger, natural setting. He worked toward this goal with many projects, including gardens at the UNESCO building in Paris, sunken plazas at the Chase Manhattan Bank building in New York and the rare book library at Yale University, and a sculpture garden at the Israel Museum in Jerusalem.

Choice of material was crucial to Noguchi. He is particularly known for his work in stone. "Stone is the fundament of the earth," he once said. "It is not old or new but a primordial element." His large stone sculptures are praised for their simple beauty. One writer said they were like three-dimensional calligraphy. Some of his stone works were even compared to ancient religious sites, like the ancient Stonehenge formation in England. Despite his fondness for stone, Noguchi also worked regularly with industrial materials like stainless steel and aluminum.

Broadened horizons to dance and theater

Perhaps unusual for a sculptor, much of Noguchi's career was spent working with choreographers, notably modern dance pioneer Martha Graham. Noguchi designed sets, costumes, and props for many productions. His gift for creating artistic envi-

Noguchi in front of the Horace E. Dodge Fountain, which he designed, in Hart Plaza in Detroit, Michigan, March 28, 1979. Reproduced by permission of UPI/Bettmann.

ronments lent itself well to the stage. Conversely, his exposure to dance inspired him to create a greater sense of movement in his sculpture. In 1948 Noguchi worked with composer Igor Stravinsky and choreographer George Balanchine on the ballet *Orpheus*. In the resulting designs, he made connections between the ancient Greek myth of Orpheus and themes in Japanese mythology.

The importance of Japanese art, literature, and culture to Noguchi's career cannot be overstated. After World War II he maintained a home in Japan and spent several months there each year. Much of his work reflects his attempts to mix the energy and restlessness of modern American life with the ancient Japanese values of simplicity and inner harmony. The best example of this is seen at the Isamu Noguchi Garden Museum, which Noguchi built in Long Island City, New York. A collection of his work is displayed there in galleries, as well as in a garden that he designed. This setting ably illustrates Noguchi's philosophies about ancient origins and modern change. There are quiet, shaded groves with benches, stone walkways, and grassy expanses. Among and around these are his powerful sculptures.

In his later years Noguchi was awarded many honors from a variety of organizations, as well as the governments of the United States and Japan. His legacy was one of synthesis, the combination of elements in order to form a whole. He brought sculpture into the worlds of architecture, landscape design, and theater. As one critic attested, "Noguchi married his easternism to the west and produced an art enriched and enlarged by both cultures."

Masterworks

1943-44	*Noodle* (marble)
1951-52	*Mu* (sandstone)
1955	*Sesshu* (aluminum)
1959	*The Roar* (marble)
1968	*Origin* (stone)
1971	*Energy Void* (granite)
1976	*Portal* (steel pipe)
1981	*Narrow Gate* (stone)
1984	*Bolt of Lightning* (stainless steel)

Georgia O'Keeffe

Born November 15, 1887
Sun Prairie, Wisconsin
Died March 6, 1986
Santa Fe, New Mexico

"One day, I found myself saying to myself … 'I can't live where I want to … go where I want to … [or] do what I want to. I can't even say what I want to.' I decided I was a stupid fool not to at least paint as I want to and say what I wanted to when I painted."

Georgia O'Keeffe spent most of her life defying social and artistic conventions. Nonetheless, her paintings have become among the most recognized and best loved of the twentieth century. Though it was considered improper in her day for a woman to become a professional artist, O'Keeffe's independence and artistic vision defied the strictures of acceptable behavior. Her work influenced several modern styles, and she has served as a role model for many women artists.

O'Keeffe was raised on a farm in Wisconsin. Her large extended family included grandparents, aunts, uncles, and six brothers and sisters. While her father, Francis O'Keeffe, farmed, her mother, Ida Totto O'Keeffe, managed the household. Ida O'Keeffe felt that the education of her children was of the utmost seriousness. In addition to their formal schooling, she spent many hours reading aloud to them, especially adventure stories like *The Arabian Nights* and popular tales of the Wild West. O'Keeffe and her sisters also received private art lessons.

Defies convention by becoming an artist

In those days young girls were expected to pursue such domestic niceties as decorative painting, quilting, and basket-making. Some women became art teachers, but few were professional artists. Indeed, most art schools had only recently begun admitting women. Young Georgia blithely ignored such social barriers; when she was 12, she announced to a friend that she was going to be an artist. From then on, she singlemindedly pursued her goal.

When O'Keeffe was 14 her family moved to Virginia. She attended several schools during this time, always taking art classes. At these schools and later at the Art Institute of Chicago, she learned traditional, European-style drawing and painting, which emphasized mimetic or "realistic" representation. O'Keeffe was very successful at this style and when she went to New York City in 1907, one of her paintings won a top prize from the Art Students League, at which she attended classes.

Lake George by Moonlight, 1924. Reproduced by permission of The Bettmann Archive.

◄ *Portrait (p. 330): Reproduced by permission of UPI/Bettmann.*

Georgia O'Keeffe

O'Keeffe could not stay in New York long. Her family's financial problems and her mother's ill health meant that she would have to earn a living on her own. She worked as a commercial illustrator in Chicago for a time and also taught art at schools in Texas, where she was fascinated by the vast, arid landscape. During the summer of 1913, O'Keeffe attended the University of Virginia, where one of her teachers introduced her to the work and thought of Russian painter **Wassily Kandinsky** (see entry). Kandinsky's ideas about music, abstract or non-representational art, and the use of color in painting appealed greatly to O'Keeffe. She felt that her work up to that time had merely followed a pre-approved model. She longed to more fully express her feelings through her art.

Fears she is going mad

Gathering her savings and canvases, O'Keeffe returned to New York. The most popular showplace there among art students was the 291 Gallery, owned by renowned photographer and artist **Alfred Stieglitz** (see entry). O'Keeffe and her fellow painters spent a lot of time at the gallery and came to respect Stieglitz as an art critic and collector of new work. But O'Keeffe was forced to leave New York temporarily in the fall of 1914 to take a job teaching at a school in South Carolina. While there she had time to ponder her work and found herself going back to simple charcoal drawings on paper. She spent many hours alone creating images unlike anything she—or anyone else— had produced before. The shapes and visions coming from her imagination worried her; she felt she might be going mad. O'Keeffe sent some of these drawings to a friend in New York who showed them to Stieglitz. He was impressed and reportedly called them the "purest, finest, sincerest things that have entered [Gallery] 291 in a long while."

This was the beginning of a long professional and personal relationship between O'Keeffe and Stieglitz, which lasted until Stieglitz's death in 1946. They were married in 1924. Stieglitz greatly encouraged O'Keeffe and used his 291 Gallery and later his American Place gallery to promote her work. He was the first to recognize the power of her uniquely personal style. He introduced her to many of the most **avant-garde** or forward-thinking artists and photographers in New York. Although she spent much time away from the city while Stieglitz remained there, they were constantly in touch.

O'Keeffe's style developed and flourished with her newfound recognition. She was enormously influenced by her surroundings: New York City, upstate New York, where Stieglitz's family had a summer home, and later New Mexico, where O'Keeffe finally settled. Her artistic debt to more traditional schools of painting, especially **impressionism,** is apparent in much of her work. But her own, singular gifts and personality conjured a truly contemporary vision from her environment; the shapes, textures, and colors of skyscrapers, skies and clouds, flowers, shells, bones, and rocks afforded her the means she sought to express an inner reality. Regarding her work in retrospect, viewers can detect modes that evolved later, such as **abstract expressionism** and **color field painting.** O'Keeffe, however, was never part of a movement or school; her fierce self-reliance and unique perspective kept her apart from any crowd.

Stirs controversy with flower paintings

Beginning in the 1920s O'Keeffe became known for her magnified, vividly colored rendering of flowers. Some observers felt that these giant blossoms, with their intimate views of the inner structures of the flora, were references to human sexual organs. O'Keeffe consistently scoffed at these interpretations, insisting it was none of her concern if the viewer chose to see such things in her paintings.

By the end of the decade O'Keeffe again began to feel discontented. As a remedy she traveled each summer to New Mexico, finding its landscapes, light, and air exceptionally stimulating. By the mid-1930s she had effectively established a permanent home near Taos, though she still spent time in New York with Stieglitz. In New Mexico she traveled and hiked through mountains and desert, gathering bones, rocks, and sticks and capturing on canvas the emotions her surroundings inspired in her. Acclaimed artists and photographers, including Eliot Porter and **Ansel Adams**

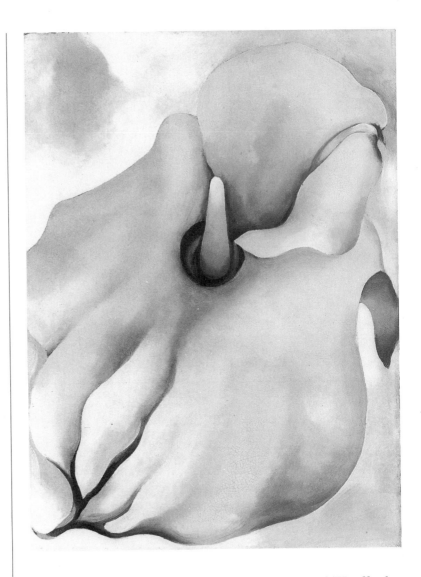

(see entry), occasionally joined her on these jaunts. O'Keeffe also found subject matter in the adobe houses and churches of the area. One of her most famous paintings from this era is *Cow's Skull: Red, White, and Blue,* which features a bleached white skull against a background of red, white, and blue. O'Keeffe labored to emphasize the exclusively American origins of her art, as opposed to drawing on the European tradition.

For the rest of her life O'Keeffe resided reclusively at her New Mexico home, which she dubbed Ghost Ranch. She painted huge canvases and took up sculpture when her eyesight began to fail. She died in 1986 at the age of 98. During much of her career, her paintings demanded large sums from collectors and museums, and she received many honors, including the Medal of Freedom, the most coveted award bestowed on a civilian in the United States. O'Keeffe left an indelible mark on history as a woman who flourished in the male-dominated field of artistic endeavor and as the possessor of a distinctive and singularly American creative vision.

Masterworks

1917	*Evening Star III*
1924	*Lake George by Moonlight*
1926	*The Shelton with Sunspots*
1928	*Oriental Poppies*
1929	*The Lawrence Tree*
1931	*Cow's Skull: Red, White, and Blue*
1935	*Blue River*
1943	*Pelvis with Moon*

I. M. Pei

Born April 26, 1917
Canton (Guangzhou), China

"It is not just a concept, but the way that concept is executed that is important."

Arguably the most celebrated of contemporary architects, I. M. Pei has designed museums, office buildings, hotels, and libraries in the United States, Europe, and Asia for more than 40 years. Rather than adhering strictly to one definable style, Pei's works fit uniquely and sometimes surprisingly into their settings. The designs for many of his structures, among them glass pyramids, shoebox-shaped concert halls, and towering skyscrapers—though often praised for their elegance and beauty of detail—have occasionally proven controversial.

He was born Ieoh Ming Pei in Canton, a city in the south of China; in Chinese his name means "to inscribe brightly." His father, Tsuyee Pei—who was descended from a prosperous family of landowners—met and married Lien Kwun Chwong while he was a university student. I. M. was the second of their five children; his father was an executive with the Bank of China in Canton at the time of his birth. The family moved to the British-ruled colony of Hong Kong when I. M. was just a year old.

During their nine years there, the boy learned English. They later moved to Shanghai, China, where Tsuyee Pei became manager of the Bank of China's main office. Shanghai was a busy, growing city, and young I. M. was fascinated by the edifices of its changing skyline, especially one that was 23 stories high.

Pei enjoyed a unique bond with his mother, who was a musician and devout Buddhist; he was profoundly affected by the retreats he took with her to Buddhist temples. She died when he was only 13 years old.

Chose architecture over medicine

Pei's father wanted him to become a doctor, but he decided instead to pursue a career in architecture, planning to study in the United States and then return to China. In 1935 Pei sailed for America, where he entered the architecture program at the University of Pennsylvania. Finding this academic environment overly conservative, and unhappy with its emphasis on drawing, he transferred to the Massachusetts Institute of Technology (MIT) and enrolled in an engineering curriculum. He excelled, and one of his professors convinced him to continue his studies in architecture. During a summer vacation, Pei drove to Wisconsin to meet one of his idols, the architect **Frank Lloyd Wright** (see entry). But he did not find Wright at his Wisconsin home and so continued driving across the country to Los Angeles, where he worked for a short time at an architectural firm. Pei received his degree in 1940.

Pei's original plan to return to China was thwarted by two political events. Japan had invaded China and war was raging there. Then, in 1941, Japan and the United States entered World War II. Pei's father advised him to stay in the United States, where he worked briefly for several architectural firms. He married Eileen Loo, who had been a college student in the Boston area when Pei was at MIT. Two of their four children eventually became architects and joined their father's firm. In 1942, as World War II continued, Pei volunteered to work for the National Defense Research Committee. He was charged with the task of researching ways to destroy buildings, an assignment he did not enjoy.

After the war Pei became a graduate student and assistant professor at Harvard University's Graduate School of Design. There he studied with two important designers, **Walter Gropius** (see entry) and Marcel Breuer. They had come to the United States from Germany, where they had founded the Bauhaus, an extremely influential school of art and modern design. Pei has said that he was especially influenced by Breuer's ideas about "light, texture, sun, and shadow." Indeed, these elements have been fundamental to Pei's work.

Communist revolution prevented return to China

After completing his master's degree, Pei hoped to return to China, but his homeland had just undergone a Communist revolution, which, once again, dashed his plans. Pei decided to remain in the States and a few years later became an American citizen. He was hired by a prominent real estate developer in New York City and tapped to head the company's architecture division, Webb & Knapp. For several years he worked on large urban projects, including private residences, office buildings, and open plaza spaces. Rarely would such a young architect be given responsibility for such large-scale assignments, but few architects are possessed of Pei's originality and creative instincts. His work rapidly established his reputation as a promising force in his field.

In the mid-1950s Pei founded his own architecture firm with three other architects from Webb & Knapp. They continued to work on city projects, earning praise for the Mile High Center in Denver, Colorado, the Place Ville-Marie in Montreal, Quebec, and the Society Hill project in Philadelphia, Pennsylvania. By the mid-1960s Pei's work was in great demand. One of his finest achievements of the period was the National Center for Atmospheric Research; located in an isolated area of Colorado, the building fit snugly into its environment, thanks to a design Pei said was influenced by the pueblo buildings of southwestern Indians. In the 1960s and early 1970s Pei also designed several art museums, including that of Syracuse, New York, as well as those at Cornell and Indiana universities.

Pei's designs have generally sprung from a project's specific demands and not from a single, signature style. Though others have scoffed at this method, he maintains that each design problem deserves a unique solution. His approach was borne out as he was hired for increasingly high-profile tasks; in 1964 Jacqueline Kennedy selected Pei as architect of the John F. Kennedy Library in Boston. The endeavor was repeatedly interrupted, however, as the site was changed three times, requiring Pei to redesign for the specifications of each location. The completed building was the object of some criticism, but it earned Pei national attention and a gold medal in 1979 from the American Institute of Architects. Another troubled project was the John Hancock Building in Boston, designed by one of Pei's partners. The skyscraper made headlines when its huge glass windows began popping out and crashing to the street below; a complicated lawsuit and tremendous publicity almost ruined Pei's firm.

But Pei's successes of the 1970s and 1980s overshadowed this debacle. His design for the East Building of the National

The East Building of the National Gallery of Art, in Washington, D.C. Courtesy of Jonathan S. Liffgens.

Masterworks

1956	Mile High Center, Denver, Colorado
1961	Government Center, Boston, Massachusetts
1967	National Center for Atmospheric Research, Boulder, Colorado
1978	National Gallery of Art, East Wing, Washington D.C.
1979	John F. Kennedy Library, Boston, Massachusetts
1982	Fragrant Hill Hotel, Beijing, China
1984	Weisner Building, MIT, Cambridge, Massachusetts
	Bank of China, Hong Kong
1989	Meyerson Symphony Center, Dallas, Texas
1989, 1993	Le Grande Louvre, Paris, France

Gallery of Art in Washington, D.C.—with its stark geometric shapes and large glass skylights—was hailed as a triumph. In the late 1970s Pei received a commission of enormous personal significance: after the opening of political relations between the United States and China, he was invited to design a hotel in the capital city, Beijing. It was the first time he had returned to China since 1935. His design combined modern comforts with numerous inspirations from the gardens and buildings he remembered from childhood. A few years later Pei designed a huge office tower for the Bank of China in Hong Kong, another personally resonant task as Pei's father had founded the original branch of the bank in that city.

Outraged some with Louvre addition

But perhaps the most significant undertaking of Pei's career began in 1983 when he was chosen by French president François Mitterand to design a major renovation and expansion of France's national museum, the Louvre. When the first phase of the project was unveiled in 1989, it was viewed by many as a spectacle. Pei had designed a new lobby, offices, and storage areas, all of them underground. But these were topped by a large glass pyramid and three smaller ones that stood right in the middle of the main courtyard of the Louvre.

Pei had diligently studied the history of the Louvre and French art and architecture, and he came to consider the triangular shape a primary symbol. He used glass so that the structure would not hide the majestic older buildings behind it, most of which had been constructed during the reign of Louis XIV. Though the appearance of this ultramodern structure amid the revered seventeenth-century buildings at first elicited howls of outrage,

within a short time the Louvre pyramid became a symbol of Paris. Critics praised its "aerial delicacy," deeming it "an exquisite object." A second phase of the Louvre renovation opened in 1993. Again Pei used geometric forms and glass to bring in light. *Time* magazine admired the way these changes in the display areas of the museum transformed "a dark and dowdy cavern to a bright and logical showcase."

Pei's most recent projects have been smaller and strikingly varied, including headquarters for one of Hollywood's top talent agencies and a bell tower for a Buddhist temple in Japan. He was also commissioned to design the Rock and Roll Hall of Fame in Cleveland, Ohio, perhaps an unusual project for a 75-year-old architect respected for his classic, clean, and tasteful designs. But the energy and inventiveness of I. M. Pei has remained a constant throughout his career, and his thoughtful, innovative work has made him a towering figure on the modern architectural landscape.

Pei's glass pyramid in the Napoleon courtyard of the Louvre Museum in Paris. Reproduced by permission of Reuters/Bettmann.

Pablo Picasso

Born October 25, 1881
Malaga, Spain
Died April 8, 1973
Mougins, France

"Not a single day without painting."

Pablo Ruiz Picasso was inspired to create art from his earliest childhood and continued to nurture and realize that inspiration until his death at the age of 93. Although he is best known for his paintings and drawings, he also produced sculpture, ceramic pieces, and book illustrations and designed costumes and scenery for the theater and ballet. Picasso's style went through a series of transformations during his long career, resulting in what art historians have come to call a variety of "periods." Most all of these were notable for the challenge they posed to traditional artistic boundaries. Picasso is considered by many to be the most influential artist of the twentieth century.

Picasso's natural artistic abilities were encouraged by his father, Jose Ruiz, a painter and art teacher. Also an influence on his art, Picasso's mother, Maria Picasso, loomed as a great presence in the young artist's emotional development as well. From about the age of 20, Picasso used only the family name of his mother, a common custom in Spain. He revealed remarkable drawing skills early on and worked often in his father's studio. Though Picasso was passionate about literature and history, he disliked formal schooling and avoided it. Nonetheless, in 1896, when he was 14, he required just one day to complete the entrance examination of the Academy of Fine Arts in Barcelona, Spain. The rules of the academy allowed one month for completion of the test.

Influenced by Spanish heritage

Picasso's work was influenced significantly by his Spanish heritage. He studied the Spanish master painters **Diego Velazquez** and **El Greco** (see entries) and remained current on social and political issues in Spain throughout his life. But perhaps the most apparent clue to the artist's powerful bond to his homeland is the appearance of Spanish cultural symbols, such as bulls and bullfighting, in much of his work.

After attending several art schools, Picasso left Spain for France in 1900. He was 19 years old. In Paris he became close to several artists who, like him, were destined to change the face of contemporary art. Among them were **Henri Matisse** (see entry), Georges Braque, Juan Gris, and Fernand Leger. He also came under the influence of many of the great artists of the late nineteenth century, including **Henri Toulouse-Lautrec, Vincent van Gogh, Claude Monet,** and **Paul Gauguin** (see entries). Some of Picasso's paintings from this early period look very much like the art of these painters, though they clearly demonstrate a distinctive style that was quickly associated with the younger artist, one that amply displayed both his talent and character.

Picasso's life in Paris was difficult, and his paintings of that era reflect this. His work from the years 1901 to 1904 are grouped into what is called his "Blue Period." The Blue Period produced paintings notable for creating a feeling of sadness in the viewer. These canvases displayed a limited range of hues and were generally bathed in blues and some greens. Many are portraits, the subjects therein thin, ghostly, and seemingly despondent.

From blue to rose

The work of the following three years, roughly 1904 to 1907, demonstrates another style shift, to what has been dubbed the "Rose Period." Many of the paintings from these years portray acrobats and circus performers. The change from dark, shadowy blues to warmer, brighter colors reflects an improvement in Picasso's fortunes; he was becoming more successful financially and was supported creatively by a stimulating circle of artistic and literary acquaintances. The friendship and patronage of writer Gertrude Stein—a portrait of whom would become one of the young painter's most famous—and her brother Leo were important factors in Picasso's growing renown.

Around 1906 Picasso's style underwent yet another metamorphosis; this time his unbridled inventiveness and innovation would make him the leader of a new school that was to change the world of art. Several elements were important to this development: first, Picasso became interested in the formal and technical aspects of drawing—how a subject is given structure on a flat page. He also was greatly moved by the popularity of **Paul Cézanne** (see entry), particularly by that painter's work of 1906 and 1907. At the same time, Matisse and others had begun studying African sculpture and ceremonial masks. These appealed to Picasso because the pieces were so different from those comprising traditional European art. Working with his friend Georges Braque, Picasso introduced a method of breaking down a subject into geometric shapes. This revolutionary approach to form became known as **cubism.**

Shocks world with cubism

One of Picasso's earliest and most famous cubist paintings, *Les Demoiselles d'Avignon,* depicts a group of five women —but in an arresting new way, one unlike any before seen in Western art. The women's bodies and faces are represented as multiple shapes. Even more astounding, Picasso had painted them from several points of view, all appearing at once spread out across the space of the canvas; somehow he had learned to present the human form in profile, three-quarters view, and

full face simultaneously. As his cubist ideas flowered, Picasso used vivid designs and colors to help viewers "decipher" the objects he had "cubed." These radical steps sent a shock wave throughout the art world. Soon other artists, such as Gris, Leger, and **Diego Rivera** (see entry) began to experiment with the

Les Demoiselles d'Avignon, 1907. Oil on canvas, 8' x 7'8". The Museum of Modern Art, New York. Reproduced by permission of AP/Wide World Photos.

345 | Pablo Picasso

What Is Cubism?

Imagine taking a sculpture of a human figure and squashing it flat so that it opens up, revealing all sides at once. Or painting a portrait of someone on a mirror and then shattering the mirror so that the person's image is broken into hundreds of shapes. These ideas can help us understand the artistic style called cubism.

What inspired Pablo Picasso, Georges Braque, and other adventurous early twentieth-century painters to create art in such a way? Cubism has its roots in the many style shifts that occurred in the roughly 50 years before Picasso unveiled his first cubist painting, *Les Demoiselles d'Avignon.* **Impressionism** and **pointillism** had explored the use of color to create space and movement. Artists like **Paul Cézanne** and **Georges Seurat** (see entries) "broke up" the canvas with dots or shapes of color. They were trying to paint the way the human eye sees—in moving "impressions." Another important inspiration for cubism was the popularity of African art, especially masks, among the young artists working in Paris at the turn of the century.

The birth of cubism is thought to have taken place in 1907, when Picasso painted his *Demoiselles.* The next year, Braque exhibited several paintings featuring the new method in an exhibition in Paris. Henri Matisse was one of the judges, and his comment on Braque's work was: "Toujours les cubes!"—"Always cubes!" It was not long before a new term, "cubism," was in widespread use, though its application was not always complimentary.

Picasso and Braque began working together in 1909 to more fully explore the style they had developed. They grappled with the basic problem of all painting and drawing: how to make an object appear three-dimensional on a flat surface. Giotto, the chief Italian painter of the pre-Renaissance era, and the artists of the **Renaissance** had used **perspective** to solve this problem. Picasso and Braque were looking for a new solution; they spent the years from about 1908 to 1914 trying to create a new way to represent the world. They hoped to express emotion, tension, and beauty by using shifting patterns of lines and shapes. The result was abstract—not realistic in the traditional sense—but in most of the paintings from these years we can recognize familiar objects, including guitars, bottles, newspapers, furniture, and fruit. This was the aim of cubism: to suggest parts and aspects of a familiar object but to let the viewer's eye and imagination fill in the rest.

Picasso and Braque and their contemporaries went on to investigate many artistic styles. But there has not been another mode in the twentieth century that so influenced such a variety of artistic pursuits—painting, sculpture, architecture, even literature. Cubism truly changed the way artists—and those of us who view their work—perceive art itself.

new style in order to express themselves in a manner that the time-honored methods could not afford them.

Picasso continued to explore cubism and other schools of painting for many years, including **surrealism,** a new classicism, and symbolism. He also developed the art of **collage,** using a variety of materials—wood, paper, cloth, yarn—for three-dimensional works. Moreover, he made constructions of cardboard and metal. As a result of this unprecedented diversity, Picasso came to be regarded as the undisputed leader among the world's artists, his technical skills and creative abilities almost universally revered.

Picasso with one of his creations, a bronze goat, at the May Salon Exhibition in Paris, May 1952. Reproduced by permisssion of UPI/Bettmann.

Guernica, 1937. Oil on canvas, 11'6" x 25'8". Museo del Prado, Madrid. © 1995 Artists Rights Society (ARS), New York/SPADEM, Paris. Giraudon/Art Resource, NY.

During World War I, Serge Diaghilev, an acclaimed Russian art critic and impresario, asked Picasso to create stage designs for his ballet troupe. The 1920s saw the artist mount several other theatrical designs. In many paintings of this period he returned to a "classical" style in which he presented the human form as massive sculpture, as if it were carved from marble. Most likely he was influenced by the many sculptures he saw during the time he spent in Italy during the war. This new style was a great contrast to the flatness of his cubist art. In the late 1920s Picasso worked with sculptor Julio Gonzales making wire sculptures.

Lashes out at war with *Guernica*

In 1937 Picasso painted what is perhaps his most famous work. During the Spanish Civil War, a small town named Guernica was destroyed by bombardment, with many people killed and injured. Picasso used his art to express his anger and grief: he painted the giant *Guernica.* He used somber colors, cubist forms, and a deep reserve of emotion to express the horror of the war. The painting, which features screaming people, mutilated corpses, flames, and injured animals, has endured as a model of antiwar sentiment.

Picasso was known for his forceful personality and colorful love life almost as much as for his work. He was also admired for letting his prodigious talents liberate his imagination; he was bound by few barriers—personal or artistic. Once he even fashioned a bull's head out of a bicycle seat and handlebars. Picasso's energy was also boundless, enabling him to work on several projects at once. "Painting is my hobby," he once said. "When I'm finished painting I paint again for relaxation."

Unlike some artists, Picasso was very shrewd in financial matters, never settling for less than he felt his work deserved. During his lifetime his work commanded the highest prices ever earned by an artist. Picasso was also a great collector; his several homes were crammed full of all sorts of objects he either bought or found—rocks, birdcages, African drums, pottery, posters, hats. He reportedly never threw anything away and allowed no one to move his things.

Even in old age, Picasso never stopped experimenting. In the 1960s, when he was in his eighties, he was commissioned by the city of Chicago to create a monument for the Civic Center Plaza. He produced a metal sculpture over six stories high that resembled some of his cubist figures. It was larger than anything he'd made before.

Picasso's genius is beyond debate. He has influenced legions of artists—sculptors, architects, writers, filmmakers, poets, and musicians, as well as painters. His numerous works can be seen in museums around the world, including the Picasso Museum in Paris, where visitors can view the work that Picasso did not share with the world during his long and fruitful life.

Masterworks

1903	*The Old Guitarist*
1904	*The Frugal Repast*
1905	*Les Saltimbanques*
	Boy Leading a Horse
1906	*Gertrude Stein*
	The Jester (sculpture)
1907	*Les Demoiselles d'Avignon*
1910	*Daniel Henry Kahnweiler*
1920	*Igor Stravinsky*
1921	*Three Musicians*
	Seated Nude
1922	*Mother and Child*
1937	*Dora Maar*
	Guernica
1964	Chicago Monument sculpture

Jackson Pollock

Born January 28, 1912
Cody, Wyoming
Died August 11, 1956
Southampton, Long Island, New York

"New needs need new techniques. The modern painter cannot express this age in the old forms of the Renaissance or of any other past culture. Each age finds its own technique."

The new technique that became painter Jackson Pollock's signature style necessitated putting his canvases on the floor and dripping, splattering, and throwing paint on them. This radical approach—with which the painter hoped to express his energetic vision—won both enthusiastic admirers and heated detractors. His life was cut short by an automobile accident when he was only 44 years old, but 40 years later his work occupies a storied place in modern painting and has been crucial to the development of a number of subsequent styles.

It is central to many of the myths surrounding Pollock's life that he was born in Wyoming, this somehow connecting him to a romantic vision of cowboys and the frontier. In fact, Pollock's family moved from Wyoming to San Diego, California, when he was just a few months old. Paul Jackson Pollock—known as Paul until he was in high school—was the youngest of Stella May McClure and LeRoy Pollock's five sons. During his childhood the poor but close-knit family moved regularly throughout California and Arizona following the demands of LeRoy Pollock's migrant farm work. Stella Pollock, known as a "capable woman who kept the family on its course," loved art and passed this passion on to her brood; all five sons eventually pursued careers in the arts.

◀ *Portrait (p. 350):* *Photograph by Hans Namuth, © The Estate of Hans Namuth.*

Expelled twice

Pollock began high school in Riverside, California, but his restless, rebellious nature prevented him from finding much of interest there; he was expelled during his first year thanks to an argument with a military recruiting officer. He attended an arts-oriented high school when the family moved to Los Angeles, where he fell under the sway of an art teacher who introduced him to Eastern mysticism, native American beliefs, and vegetarianism. But Pollock was expelled again, along with two friends, this time for publishing a pamphlet criticizing the school for encouraging and rewarding athletics at the expense of academics; nonetheless, he was readmitted the next year.

By this time two of Pollock's older brothers—who were studying art in New York—had begun sending him enticing clippings and academic news. When they came home for a visit in the summer of 1930, Pollock decided to accompany them on their return. He spent two years at the prestigious Art Students League, mostly studying with Thomas Hart Benton, who had gained a sizable reputation for his "American realism"—depictions of working people, particularly cowboys. Pollock helped mix paints for Benton and posed for some of his works.

Pollock had yet to definitively decide on a career. He felt that he had some talent, but he was uncertain about his technical abilities and the expressive capacity of his work. Fortunately, Benton recognized Pollock's potential and encouraged him; the two corresponded long after the younger artist had moved on. Benton wrote to Pollock, "You've the stuff old kid—all you have to do is keep it up."

The 1930s marked an exciting period in art, despite the crushing economic conditions of the Great Depression. In 1934 and 1935 Pollock was earning ten dollars a week working as a school janitor, sharing his meager salary with one of his brothers. In 1935, however, he was accepted into the Federal Art Project, a government aid program, and was paid about $90 a month to turn in a handful of paintings per year. This income was vital to Pollock's development; it enabled him to take classes, in which he met other young artists.

Experimented with new techniques

In 1936 Pollock worked in the studio of Mexican artist David Siqueiros, renowned for his **mural** wall paintings. His workshop was the site of considerable experimentation: budding artists investigated new tools like spray-paint guns and airbrushes, as well as innovations in synthetic paint. This open, exploratory atmosphere stimulated Pollock's imagination. He also found inspiration in frequent road trips across the country, sketching the sprawling landscapes of the West during his travels.

Pollock's work from this era betrays a restless search for his signature style. Many of his canvases echo the dark outlines and strong forms of the Mexican style embodied by Siqueiros and Mexican social realist **Diego Rivera.** Other paintings employed abstract forms reminiscent of Spanish painter and sculptor **Pablo Picasso,** whose work Pollock studied with great intensity, as he did the creations of Russian master of the abstract **Wassily Kandinsky** (see entries), to whom he was introduced during his tenure as a custodian at New York City's Museum of Non-Objective Painting (later the Solomon R. Guggenheim Museum). Pollock's work appeared in several government-sponsored shows throughout the country, yet despite the comforts of financial aid and some small success, Pollock suffered emotionally. Beginning in the late 1930s, he underwent treatment for alcoholism and psychological difficulties. Though he sporadically controlled his drinking problem, it is widely believed that alcohol played a role in the auto accident that ended his life.

In 1941 Pollock's work formed part of an important New York gallery exhibit, where it was noticed by another young artist, Lee Krasner. Krasner, after discovering that Pollock lived around the corner from her, sought him out; thus began an artis-

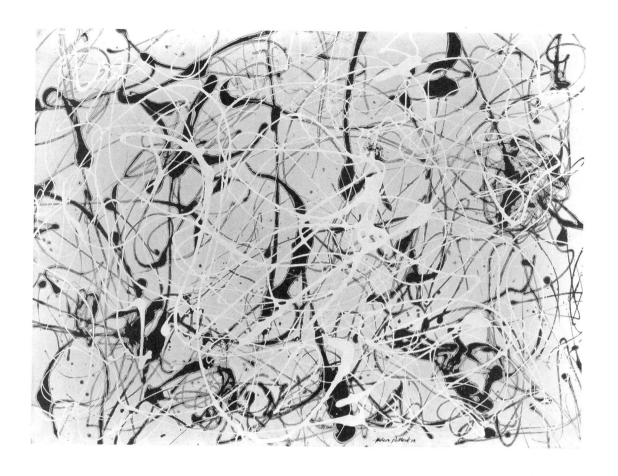

Number 23, 1948.
Tate Gallery, London.
© 1995 Pollock-Krasner
Foundation/Artists Rights
Society (ARS), New York.
Tate Gallery/Art Resource,
NY.

tic partnership that led to marriage and lasted until Pollock's death. Krasner introduced Pollock to other artists and provided him with indispensable psychological support. By 1942 he had begun to define the contours of his mature style: his outsized, vividly colored new canvases were strewn with symbols. Paintings like *Male and Female* and *The Moon-Woman* displayed the swirling energy of shapes and lines that became typical of Pollock's work, as well as his celebrated "alloverness," characterized by a rejection of central focus in favor of spreading designs all over the canvas.

The wealthy and powerful collector-exhibitor Peggy Guggenheim took a singular interest in Pollock's work, sponsoring his first solo exhibit at her gallery in 1943 and three more shows from 1945 to 1947. Pollock's efforts were the object of extravagant praise—and stern disapproval from critics who la-

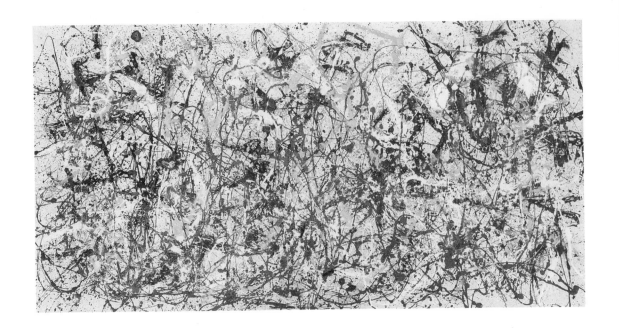

Autumn Rhythm: Number 30, 1950. *Oil on canvas, 8'9" x 17'3". The Metropolitan Museum of Art, New York. George A. Hearn Fund, 1957 (57.92).*

beled it "lavish, explosive, and undisciplined." An unanswered question in many reviews pertained to the degree of control this firebrand really exercised in his works.

Laid canvases on barn floor

Pollack had bought a house and barn on Long Island with Krasner, using the barn for his studio and tacking his paintings to the floor instead of working on an easel. "On the floor I am more at ease," he wrote in 1947. "I feel nearer, more a part of the painting, since ... I can walk around it, work from the four sides and literally be in the painting." At this point Pollock began to lay snaking lines of paint over some of the images in his paintings to veil or hide them. He found in this technique the key to the next phase of his work; he gave up the "background" and began painting only the "veil" of squiggling, spattering drips and lines.

Pollock made use of a variety of unusual implements to achieve his desired effects, including hardened brushes, trowels, sticks, and even kitchen staples like basters. He used his wrists, arms, and whole body as he whirled thin streams of paint around the canvas. He would drip one color at a time, waiting until the previous one had dried. He tried out different kinds and thicknesses of paint, including metallics. The surface would become interwoven with colored lines, often seeming to explode with its vibrant hues and untrammeled creative verve.

Pollock improvised his canvases, not bothering with sketches or plans and thus inviting the charge that he merely painted chaos. When an interviewer asked him if he had an image in his mind before he began, Pollock replied, "Well, not exactly ... because it hasn't been created, you see.... I do have a general notion of what I'm about and what the results will be." He used the paint to draw—a revolutionary idea at the time given the standard method of using paint to finalize what had first been drawn—since he found in this an appropriate means for manifesting his emotions. "When I am *in* my painting," he wrote, "I'm not aware of what I am doing. It is only after a sort of 'get acquainted' period that I see what I have been about ... because the painting has a life of its own."

Landmark development or child's play?

Critics in the late 1940s were widely divided about the new form that Pollack was spearheading; it became known as **abstract expressionism,** or action painting. When Pollock's works appeared in exhibitions, some praised them as a landmark development in modern art, while others derided the pieces as empty and merely decorative. Some critics condemned the canvases as too random and argued that any child could drip paint and get similar results. Yet scores of viewers have found meaning in Pollock's creation of space or lack thereof through the use of his drips and lines and the very texture of paint on the canvas. Most of Pollock's works from this time bear only numbers and dates as titles, as he rapidly abandoned descriptive labels. In the 1950s, though, he did bestow a few evocative names, like *Autumn Rhythm* and *Lavender Mist.*

Pollock continued experimenting with his style into the 1950s, working for a time exclusively in black and white. Later, specific faces, figures, and animals began to appear in his paintings. Toward the mid-1950s Pollock even combined his drip tech-

Masterworks

1942	*Male and Female*
1943	*Composition with Pouring II*
1944	*Totem Lesson 1*
1946	*Eyes in the Heat*
1948	*Number 13A, 1948: Arabesque*
1950	*Lavender Mist: Number 1, 1950*
	Autumn Rhythm, Number 30, 1950
1952	*Blue Poles: Number 11, 1952*
1953	*Easter and the Totem*

nique with traditional brushwork. Works like *Easter and the Totem* and *Ocean Greyness* garnered praise for their variety and inventiveness and demonstrated the artist's capacity to grow and change. Pollock's work appeared in exhibitions throughout the world and powerfully influenced that of other artists. **Helen Frankenthaler** (see entry) developed yet another mode of painting, the soak-stain technique, after seeing, and being amazed by, Pollock at work in his studio.

A crash on a curving Long Island road brought an end to this promising career. A few months before his death, a large show of Pollock's works had opened at an important New York gallery. He had created, according to one critic, "the most original art among the painters of his generation." Indeed, he would cast a prominent shadow over the artists who followed him. "There was a reviewer a while back who wrote that my pictures didn't have any beginning or any end," Pollock once told a writer for the *New Yorker.* "He didn't mean it as a compliment, but it was ... a fine compliment." Even four decades after Pollock's death, the story begun by his work goes on.

Rembrandt van Rijn

Born July 15, 1606
Leiden, Netherlands

Died October 4, 1669
Amsterdam, Netherlands

Rembrandt is renowned as one of the world's great paint-ers of portraits and self-portraits. Indeed, his artistic skills came easily; by the time he was 25, he was already a popu-lar, established painter in Amsterdam. But it is not necessarily Rembrandt's technical abilities that are best remembered; his work is most appreciated for the depth of emotion, vitality, and personality that he revealed. His approximately 600 portraits and over 1,000 drawings and **etchings** offer us a lively picture of life in seventeenth-century Holland and set a lofty standard for the portrait painters who followed him.

Rembrandt van Rijn's parents, Harmen and Cornelia van Rijn, enjoyed a comfortable life raising their nine children in the town of Leiden. Harmen van Rijn was a miller, his chief occupation grinding grain into flour for local farmers. Rembrandt attended grammar school and later briefly pursued studies at the nearby university, but he always knew he would be an artist. He worked as an apprentice, or assistant, to a local painter for

"Apart from his immense gifts as a pure painter and an illustrator, Rembrandt digs down to the roots of life; and he seems to open his heart to us. We have the feeling he is keep-ing nothing back."

Kenneth Clark

roughly three years. During this time he drew and painted portraits of his parents and many of the people of the area. Throughout his life Rembrandt had great sympathy for those who were hungry and homeless; he made his living painting portraits of prosperous merchants and doctors, but his eye was drawn to ordinary folk, who he thought were more real and thus infinitely more interesting. Pages of his drawings are filled with street vendors, beggars, African slaves, and unremarkable citizens going about their daily lives.

Middle class clamors for portraits

Rembrandt went to Amsterdam when he was about 20 years old. It was a bustling city, the largest port in Europe, with ships arriving constantly from all over the world. These vessels brought wonderful and exotic items—paintings from Italy, carpets and draperies from the Middle East, cloth and spices from India. Rembrandt collected such delicacies, often using them as props in his paintings. The busy commerce of Amsterdam led to the growth of a solid middle class, people with comfortable incomes, such as bankers, merchants, doctors, and city officials. This group was sufficiently well off to enjoy the arts and to have their portraits painted. The growing popularity of portraiture was convenient for a young painter new to the city.

The art of the Italian **Renaissance**—the paintings and sculpture of great masters like **Michelangelo** and **Leonardo da Vinci** (see entries), who had lived only about a hundred years earlier—was all the rage in Amsterdam in these years. Friends urged Rembrandt to investigate the many Italian paintings and drawings on display there. He did study briefly with an Italian-trained artist and probably saw and was influenced by the works of **Titian** (see entry), Raphael, and Caravaggio and those painters' mastery of color, light, and composition. But Rembrandt was not one to adopt another artist's style; even in his mid-twenties, his talent was unique and self-assured. Word quickly spread about this able young painter from Leiden, and Rembrandt soon had many commissions from individuals and groups.

The first group or "corporate" portrait he was hired to paint presents an assembly of students gathered around a cadaver while a doctor teaches them anatomy. *The Anatomy Lesson of Dr. Tulp* was painted when Rembrandt was only 26, but it clearly demonstrates his expressive use of light and shadow, with the men's bright white collars seeming to illuminate their faces and a light from above highlighting the body. Dr. Tulp was very pleased with the painting and hung it prominently in his school of surgery. Many heard of the work, and Rembrandt's popularity grew.

Transforms the ordinary with clever use of light

The individuals who hired Rembrandt to paint them were the prosperous and usually conservative citizens of Amsterdam. They are portrayed in many of his portraits, their black clothing and hats and starched white collars indicating the plain and serious people they were. Yet Rembrandt added interest to the portraits with small details and dramatic lighting to lend character and life to the subject. Perhaps as a reaction to painting so many somber, darkly clad figures, Rembrandt often painted himself, friends, and his wife, Saskia, dressed in fancy hats, capes, turbans, helmets, and embroidered draperies. His gift for mastering color and light with his pigments added sparkle to jewelry and metal and a sheen to satin and silk. The richness of such touches is typical of a Rembrandt painting.

Throughout the course of his life, Rembrandt completed roughly 60 self-portraits, sometimes in elaborate costume, other times just to record his own image. These give us the opportunity to see how he changed over the years. Early self-portraits paint him as an eager, energetic young man, often dressed in the hats, armor, and capes he collected. Later in life he appears heavier, more serious, and even in bad temper—a complex person who has led a varied life. Each self-portrait seems sincere and truthful, each lit by its own beauty.

Rembrandt was at the height of his success and wealth in 1642 when Saskia died, leaving the painter alone to raise their son, Titus, who was less than a year old. Three other children had died as infants. Despite his prominence, financial difficul-

ties and health problems as well seemed to multiply during the 1640s and 1650s. Ironically, many of his most prized works were painted during these decades. Possibly the most famous is *The Militia Company of Captain Frans Banning Cocq,* more often called *The Night Watch.* This scene of a military company, with their swords, guns, drums, and banners, is loaded with action. The dramatic light shining on the two central figures lends a gripping focus to the painting. But some members of the regiment were unhappy that their faces were in shadow, and they refused to pay Rembrandt their portion of his fee. To be sure, the artist was not primarily interested in them; he was concentrating on the structure and drama of the work as a whole. When the painting was hung in their regiment hall in Amsterdam, one of Rembrandt's pupils wrote that it was "so powerful that all the other pieces there stand beside it like mere playing cards."

Lent local folk and settings to biblical scenes

When Rembrandt was not painting commissioned works, his favorite pastimes were painting or drawing religious scenes and sketching the people and neighborhoods of the city. His interpretations of biblical narratives, often the stories of the Old Testament, were deeply personal. He used the sketches he had made of people he saw in Amsterdam as models, often depicting them dressed in the Dutch clothes of their time and in local settings around the city. He did this to emphasize the importance of the emotion contained in the Bible tales; to him, it was insignificant that Abraham or Samson or Jesus was not dressed in the ancient style. As Rembrandt got older and faced increasing problems in his life, his religious works seemed to become even more intense and beautiful.

One famous non-religious painting from this period is *Aristotle Contemplating a Bust of Homer,* which portrays the famous Greek philosopher resting his hand on the sculpted representation of the ancient poet. Rembrandt has given the face of

◀ Rembrandt and Saskia, *1634. Oil on canvas, 5′ 3½″ x 4′ 3½″. Gemäldegalerie, Dresden. Reproduced by permission of Alinari/Art Resource, NY.*

Aristotle and the head of Homer a golden glow, honoring them and acknowledging his connection to them in their concern with truth and the nature of humankind.

In 1656 Rembrandt, deeply in debt, was forced to sell his large home, where he maintained his studio, painted and taught many students, and kept his large collections of art, ancient armor, costumes, jewels, and other treasures. His son Titus, by then a teenager, and his longtime companion, Hendrickje Stoffels, who had posed for many paintings, moved with him to a small hotel in a poor area of Amsterdam. Rembrandt's money troubles continued, his eyesight began to fail, and he often suffered from illness and hunger, yet he continued to paint religious scenes, self-portraits, and landscapes of the

Dutch countryside, most of them from his imagination. His last years were very hard, though there were great moments like the visit in 1668 from the Grand Duke of Tuscany, a descendant of the Medici family, who had been patrons of Michelangelo and other Renaissance artists. The duke had heard of Rembrandt's artistry and came to secure one of his paintings. While the art world seemed to appreciate this master, he nonetheless died in poverty, with only his art materials and some clothes to his name.

Rembrandt's enormous talent lay in two aspects of his art: first, his ability to manipulate paint to make the viewer almost feel the richness of clothing, jewelry, and hair. He virtually sculpted with his brushes and thick paints. The second of Rembrandt's primary skills was his gift for capturing energy and emotion in even the most sedate scenes or portraits. Feeling came through his pen or brush in his contrasts of light and dark, in the structure of his compositions, and in his use of real people for models. He was far ahead of his time in his interest in color as a tool and in his fascination with the common folk. Three hundred years later, the impressionists, among them the great painters **Claude Monet** and **Pierre-Auguste Renoir** (see entries), revived and extended these ideas.

Masterworks

1634	*The Anatomy Lesson of Dr. Tulp*
	Rembrandt and Saskia
1638	*Samson Threatening His Father-in-Law*
1642	*The Night Watch*
1650	*Christ Healing the Sick (Hundred Guilder Print)*
1654	*Aristotle Contemplating a Bust of Homer*
1655	*The Polish Rider*
1656	*Titus Reading*
1662	*The Board of the Clothmakers Guild*
1665	*The Jewish Bride*

Pierre-Auguste Renoir

Born February 25, 1841
Limoges, France
Died December 3, 1919
Cagnes, France

"For me a picture ... should be something likeable, joyous and pretty.... There are enough ugly things in life for us not to add to them."

The paintings of Pierre-Auguste Renoir and his close friend Claude Monet are prime examples of the style known as **impressionism.** These two artists belonged to the group of French painters who departed from traditional methods and sought a new way of viewing the world by virtue of a more emotionally direct use of light and color. Renoir remains one of the most admired impressionists; his sun-filled paintings of bathers, children, flowers, and river boats are full of joy and optimism.

Renoir was the sixth child of a working-class family from Limoges, France; his father struggled to earn a living for the family as a tailor. The clan moved to Paris when Renoir was three years old. By age 13 he was working in a porcelain china factory painting flowers on dishes. He learned to imitate the ornate French **rococo** style of the eighteenth century, became adept at producing decorative fans, and was eventually hired to depict scenes from mythology on the walls of cafés around Paris.

Helps develop impressionism

But by the time he was about 19, Renoir had become dissatisfied with his work. He had saved enough money to pay for a year's study in a master's studio, and though he found the teaching dull, he met several students there who would become lifelong friends and colleagues. Renoir, Alfred Sisley, Jean Bazille, and **Claude Monet** (see entry) formed the core of forward-thinkers who founded the impressionist movement; they spent hours in cafés discussing color and how to paint light. They were powerfully influenced by the revolutionary ideas of the older, more experienced artist **Edouard Manet** (see entry), who joined their round table. What's more, all of these painters found inspiration in Japanese woodblock prints, which had begun to appear in Europe in the mid-1850s.

During the 1860s and 1870s, Renoir and Monet worked together quite often, sometimes sitting side by side and painting the same scene. They were both interested in open-air painting—*plein air* in French—and carefully observed the effects of sunlight and weather on their environment; they found that laying broad dashes of vivid color on their canvases mimicked the effects of sunlight when viewed from a distance. In the summer of 1869, the two painters went to a popular resort called La Grenouillère, which lay on the River Seine near Paris. Monet and Renoir's paintings of this setting are among the first to demonstrate the key elements of impressionism. While his fellow impressionists largely occupied themselves with landscapes and other *plein air* or outdoor pursuits, Renoir preferred human subjects; even his outdoor views usually have people in them. He displayed a special fondness for depictions of leisure—everyday folk engaged in boating, swimming, taking a meal, reading, or playing music.

These early impressionist paintings puzzled both critics and the public, so few of them were sold. As a result, Renoir suffered through hard times, but he was eventually able to support himself by painting portraits. By 1874 the impressionist ranks had swelled to include, among others, **Paul Cézanne** (see entry), Edgar Degas, Berthe Morisot, and Camille Pissarro. They decided to hold a collective exhibition and mounted eight such shows over the next 12 years. The first of these occasioned a critic's horrified exclamation that Monet's painting *Impression: Sunrise* was not a painting but merely an "impression"; despite the unfavorable cast of this remark, the maverick assemblage of artists subsequently began calling themselves impressionists.

Dappled and sparkling light

The 1870s and first half of the 1880s marked a deeply creative and successful period for Renoir. One of his most famous

paintings, *Le Moulin de la Galette,* is often considered the ultimate impressionist work. It presents a group of people in the
garden of a large café dancing, talking, drinking, and enjoying
themselves. The dappled and sparkling light coming through
the trees above them and from the lanterns in the garden high-
light a hat here, a woman's skirt there; the work dances with
movement and color. The viewer can see in it conventions of the
eighteenth-century paintings Renoir copied as a youth, mod-
ernized with the characters and fashions of his own time and
energized by the stylistic imperatives of impressionism.

A few years later, Renoir painted *The Luncheon of the
Boating Party,* another classic of impressionism; it portrays a
jolly gathering at an outdoor restaurant. The wine glasses
sparkle, as do the white clothes of the participants, amply con-
veying to viewers the warmth and joyousness of the occasion.

*Le Moulin de la Galette,
1876. Oil on canvas,
4′ 3½″ x 5′ 9″. Louvre, Paris.
Reproduced by permission of
Giraudon/Art Resource, NY.*

One of the women featured in the painting later became Renoir's wife.

In the early 1880s Renoir began traveling to numerous locales in Europe and North Africa. In Italy he studied the paintings of Raphael and other **Renaissance** artists; the works of **Rembrandt van Rijn** in Holland and of **Diego Velazquez** and **Francisco Goya** (see entries) in Spain also interested him greatly. He commented at length in his writings on the brilliant sunlight and rich colors he found in North Africa. Yet all of these new influences brought Renoir to a kind of crisis in his work. He wrote, "I had gone to the end of Impressionism and I was reaching the conclusion that I didn't know how either to paint or to draw." Studying the great painters of the past inspired him to pursue new ideas in his art: from the mid-1880s into the 1890s, Renoir's paintings show him experimenting with more linear styles, more classical poses, and a fresh palette of colors.

Continues to paint despite arthritis

In 1890 Renoir married Aline Charigot. She and the couple's three children—and even their nanny—became frequent subjects for Renoir and can often be recognized by their beautiful red hair. By this point Renoir's paintings were in great demand, and by 1900 he had achieved such a level of renown that the French government awarded him the coveted Legion of Honor medal. At the same time, however, he began suffering from arthritis, a painful joint disease, which sometimes made it difficult for him to hold a paintbrush; yet he did not stop painting—sometimes even tying the brush to his hand. He turned with increasing frequency to studies of women, who were often depicted nude and reclining or bathing in rivers. A painting from 1918, *The Bathers,* is characterized by the lush-looking, almost touchably soft skin of the subjects and the reddish hue for which Renoir became known.

Renoir's last few years were difficult. By 1910 he was permanently confined to a wheelchair. His wife died in 1915, and two of his sons were injured in World War I. He saw increasing fame and success, however, and in 1917 began to receive regular visits from **Henri Matisse** (see entry); he was intrigued by Matisse's style, which was called **fauvism.** In 1919 one of Renoir's paintings was purchased by the Louvre, the French national museum. He was able to visit his painting there and see it hanging among the great works of the past. It was his final honor; he died a few months later at the age of 78.

Renoir's paintings have sustained the admiration of art lovers throughout this century. Although his works are sometimes criticized for not being "serious" enough, the delicacy of his brushwork and his love of the human figure make the paintings irresistibly warm, lively, and undeniably appealing. Indeed, Renoir once remarked, "For me a picture ... should be something likable, joyous and pretty.... There are enough ugly things in life for us not to add to them."

Masterworks

1869	*La Grenouillère*
1873	*Monet Painting in His Garden at Argenteuil*
1876	*Le Moulin de la Galette*
1878	*Madame Charpentier and Her Children*
1880-81	*Luncheon of the Boating Party*
1881-86	*Les Parapluies (The Umbrellas)*
1882	*Le Danse a Bougival*
1887	*The Bathers*
1896	*Girls at the Piano*
1905	*Claude Renoir Playing*
1918-19	*The Bathers*

Faith Ringgold

Born October 8, 1930
New York, New York

"The fact that I'm considered a minority on every count frees me to do what I want to do. I believe in being an artist as a way of life; my intention is serious, and I'm ready to challenge anyone who says what I do isn't."

Faith Ringgold calls herself "a painter who works in the quilt medium." Hers is a unique and easily recognizable style. She has worked in oil painting, traditional sculpture, and watercolors, but she is indeed best known for her soft sculptures and story quilts. Her political activity of the 1960s and 1970s galvanized her artistic approach. Many of her works address the experiences of African American women past and present, and despite their serious message, they have been generally described as lively, imaginative, and humorous. Most recently, Ringgold has been acclaimed as the author and illustrator of several children's books.

Ringgold grew up in New York City's predominantly black Harlem section. She remembers it as a place with a strong sense of community. "It was a highly protective place. Almost an extended family," she wrote. Her father, Andrew Louis Jones, drove a truck for the New York City Sanitation Department and her mother, Willi Posey Jones, was a fashion designer and seamstress. The family, which included Ringgold's older brother and sister, lived a comfortable life, despite the hard economic times of the 1930s.

Asthma the catalyst to artistic development

When Ringgold was two years old, she developed asthma and was thereafter forced to spend much of her time in bed. This limitation was key to her development as an artist. "I was making things in my bed: drawings, watercolors, all kinds of things," she recalls. Her mother showed her many of the ways in which she could use fabric in these projects.

When Ringgold was still very young her parents separated. Her mother continued working and took on full responsibility for raising the three children. Because she was too sick to regularly attend school, Ringgold was taught at home by her mother. Willi Jones took her daughter to museums or the theater, where she saw many of the great performers of the era, among them jazz singer Ella Fitzgerald, singer and actress Judy Garland, and bandleader Duke Ellington. Ringgold dreamed of being someone important when she grew up.

When her health improved, Ringgold resumed formal schooling. Her classmates admired her artwork and often asked her to help them with special projects. During high school she began drawing portraits of family members and friends; she remembers that they often grew weary of posing and sometimes were not pleased with the results. She kept practicing anyway. But it wasn't until after graduation from high school in 1948 that Ringgold seriously considered a career in art. She applied to the City College of New York (CCNY), though women were not admitted to the liberal arts college in those days. She could, however, study art through the school of education. Since her grandparents and other relatives had been teachers, Ringgold felt this would be a suitable path for her as well; she could teach art and continue her own work in her free time.

At CCNY Ringgold copied classical sculpture, studied the French artists Edgar Degas and **Paul Cézanne** (see entry), and secured "a sound background in Western art." Though she did well, she also remembers frustration with the traditional art classes. "I wanted something more. I didn't know how to get from Degas and the Greek busts ... to Faith. That would take me considerable time." Her teachers disapproved when she tried to inform her work with personal experience; they would not even help her mix paints so that she could approximate the skin tone of African Americans.

European tradition obscured African American heritage

Ringgold's work at CCNY was disrupted when she married Robert Earl Wallace, a musician. By the time she was 22, she had two daughters. She went back to school and finished her bachelor's degree in 1955; she then began her 18-year teaching career in the New York public schools. After her marriage ended, Ringgold returned to school and earned a master's degree in 1959. It was then that she began to consider a full-time career as an artist. After a trip to Europe visiting museums with her mother and daughters, Ringgold's mind was made up; she set up a studio at home and began painting in earnest. Her second husband, Burdette Ringgold, helped her by making the rounds of galleries with her work. But gallery owners reacted negatively to traditional, European-style paintings by an African American woman. This reminded Ringgold of her futile attempts at school to insert herself into her art. The problem, she ascertained, was that she had "no knowledge about the visual arts of black people. I appreciated the beauty of European art.... But I understood that that wasn't my heritage."

The 1960s were a time of great social and political upheaval for African Americans. Ringgold was influenced by the writings of several black authors and artists whose works were defining the civil rights era, including collagist **Romare Bearden** and painter **Jacob Lawrence** (see entries). As the 1960s progressed, Ringgold began to incorporate her political convictions into her art. In 1967 she painted *U.S. Postage Stamp Commemorating the Advent of Black Power.* It was a huge postage stamp,

Tar Beach (Woman on Beach Series #1), 1988. Acrylic paint on canvas bordered with printed and painted quilted and pieced cloth, 74⅝" x 68½". Solomon R. Guggenheim Museum, New York. Gift of Mr. and Mrs. Gus and Judith Lieber, 1988. Reproduced by permission of David Heald. Copyright The Solomon R. Guggenheim Foundation, New York (FN 88.3620).

with a grid of white and African American faces. Letters spelling out "White Power" and "Black Power" helped define the latticework. With this piece Ringgold longed to express her feelings about race relations.

During the late 1960s and early 1970s, another powerful political force influenced Ringgold: the women's movement. She became very active, taking part in many protests to promote equality for women, especially in the art world. Her efforts helped put more works by women and African Americans in museums and galleries. Her own work was earning attention as well. In 1971 she received a grant to paint a **mural** at the prison for women on Riker's Island near New York. She painted a scene intended to inspire the inmates. It depicted women of many backgrounds pursuing a variety of careers, from police officer to priest to musician—even a woman as president.

Inspired by disappointed student

A 1973 incident rerouted Ringgold's focus from wider social issues to more personal ones. One of her students visited an exhibit of her work and told Ringgold that she was disappointed. "I didn't see any of the techniques you teach us," the student complained. Ringgold realized that none of her own works used the African techniques she taught her students, such as beadwork, tie-dying, and cloth sculpture. This was a turning point in Ringgold's career. Her work blossomed, and since then she has become one of the foremost artists in the medium of cloth.

Ringgold began using the sewing and needlework skills her mother had taught her to create masks and cloth figures. The first were modeled on relatives and women in her neighborhood. She decorated them with beadwork, paint, and embroidery. The life-size African-style masks were often rendered with their mouths open to symbolize the rich storytelling tradition of African culture. These were "portraits" of strong women who served as the artist's role models. She also fashioned masks of children, homeless people, and heroes like civil rights leader Martin Luther King, Jr. Ringgold eventually began to attach clothing or robes to the masks so that they could be worn as costumes.

On another trip to Europe, Ringgold came into contact with *tankas,* Tibetan cloth frames made for sacred paintings. She soon began producing *tankas* for her own paintings. Their bright colors beautifully offset her work and enabled canvases to be rolled up and carried around. At about this time Ringgold gave up teaching and began to travel to colleges to offer workshops, lecture, and show her works. She also produced theater performances to accompany some of her pieces. One, *The Wake and Resurrection of the Bicentennial Negro,* employed cloth figures to dramatize the "resurrection" of a drug addict and his wife who become drug-free and spiritually liberated. "I was trying to point up what happened to [African Americans] in the 200 years of our country, and the resurrection was meant to say, let it not happen again," Ringgold told the *New York Times.*

Established quilting specialty

To help with her cloth works, Ringgold called on her mother, Willi Jones, whose career in sewing and fashion design had by then spanned several decades. They designed a quilt for a 1983 exhibition called "The Artist and the Quilt." Eighteen artists designed and assembled quilts for this show. Ringgold's contribution was her first effort in the medium; it served as a gallery of faces from her Harlem neighborhood. Ringgold's mother died before the exhibition took place. After much grief-stricken soul searching, she decided that continuing her work with cloth and quilts would best honor her mother.

During the mid-1980s, in fact, many of Ringgold's paintings looked like quilts. Scenes and figures were made of shapes resembling cloth cutouts, and she included borders around the compositions as one would find in quilting. Sometimes she even stitched through the painted canvas in order to lend it the body of a quilt. One such work, *Groovin' High,* is a dance scene that features figures kicking their legs and moving in all directions on a floor of black and white squares. The movement and rhythm considerably enliven the canvas. In *Who's Bad?*, Ringgold celebrated the music and dance of pop star Michael Jackson. He is shown dancing on a floor festooned with the names of famous African Americans. Behind him are dancers who leap, twist, and sway to the music.

As Ringgold's prominence gained momentum and her confidence instilled ever more freedom of expression, she longed to better communicate with her viewers. Thus were born her story quilts. She initiated a new method in which a story was told around the quilted edges of the pictures she painted. One of her first story quilts, called *Church Picnic,* narrates the love of a young woman and a minister in a southern town around 1900. Imagination, memories, and stories told to her by relatives served in the creation of the scene. Several of Ringgold's quilts illustrate the importance of mealtime in African American homes. *Harlem Renaissance Party* portrays a dinner table surrounded by famous artists and writers of 1930s Harlem; included are activist W. E. B. Du Bois, writer Countee Cullen, and folklorist Zora Neale Hurston. Ringgold's art celebrates the rich heritage left by these creative people.

Black women visit van Gogh's sunflowers

In 1991 Ringgold visited Paris again and began work on a series of 12 story quilts called "The French Collection." Through these she told the tale of a young African American artist who visits many of the famous European masters of the past, among them **Henri Matisse** and **Vincent van Gogh** (see entries). In one work, *The Sunflowers Quilting Bee at Arles,* Ringgold again elevates African American culture, while also revealing her love of European painting. She presents a group of famous black women at a quilting bee in a field of sunflowers like those painted frequently by van Gogh at Arles, in southeastern France. Van Gogh himself stands nearby watching them.

Ringgold's most recent endeavor is book illustration. Though she has illuminated stories by other authors, her own book, *Tar Beach,* became a best-seller and won the Caldecott

Honor Book Award and the Coretta Scott King Illustrator Award in 1992. It centers on an African American girl who dreams of flying from the rooftop of her apartment building in New York out over the city. Ringgold based the story on memories of her family spending summer evenings on the roof of their building. The tale expresses Ringgold's hope that all people will follow their dreams and resist the ugliness of racism and sexism. Indeed, one reviewer commented that Ringgold blends imagination, color, and composition to demonstrate values like freedom, justice, love, and the triumph of the human spirit. Among the artist's other books are *Aunt Harriet's Underground Railroad in the Sky* and *Dinner at Aunt Connie's House.*

Aside from pursuing her career in the visual and tactile arts, Ringgold has returned to teaching, becoming a university professor. She has received many laurels for her work, including six honorary degrees from a variety of colleges and universities. Her accomplishments are all the more remarkable because she was forced to pursue a path in art largely untested by black women and as such, spent years breaking down the dictates of tradition in order to preserve her personal vision. To be sure, Ringgold doggedly followed her childhood dream of being someone important, and today her works hang in museums and stand on bookshelves the world over.

Masterworks

1967	*U.S. Postage Stamp Commemorating the Advent of Black Power* (painting)
1975	*Martin Luther King* (cloth sculpture)
1983	*"Dah"* (painting; series)
1986	*Harlem Renaissance Party* (painting and cloth)
1988	*Who's Bad?* (painting and cloth)
1991	*"French Collection"* (story quilts)
	Tar Beach (book)

Diego Rivera

Born December 8, 1886
Guanajuato, Mexico
Died November 24, 1957
Mexico City, Mexico

"For the first time in the history of art, Mexican mural painting made the masses the hero of monumental art ... the man of the fields, of the factories, of the cities, and towns."

Diego Rivera's many contributions to contemporary art include the revival of the fresco in his mural paintings and the increasing valuation of Mexican **folk art** in "high" culture. Rivera's artistic genius and political beliefs gained him great acclaim and notoriety during his lifetime, and his legacy has been a growing interest among artists in putting their work to use in the service of social and political activism.

Diego Maria Rivera and his twin brother were born in 1886 to Diego Rivera and Maria Barrientos de Rivera in the small mining town of Guanajuato, northwest of Mexico City. Diego Rivera senior worked as a schoolteacher, local government official, and editor of a small newspaper. His involvement in local politics and concern for the plight of the poor and working people of Mexico influenced the younger Rivera throughout his life.

Diego Rivera soon revealed himself to be a bright, observant child, who also happened to get into trouble. By age four he was spending much of his time drawing—often on any available surface, including furniture and walls. His father covered the walls of one room in the family home with canvas and gave Diego drawing materials; this was his first studio. His favorite subjects were machines and trains, which figured prominently in his later work.

◀ *Portrait (p. 378):* *Reproduced by permission of The Bettmann Archive.*

Child prodigy

Diego's beloved great-aunt read to him from his father's library and introduced him to her collection of Mexican folk art, which cast a peculiar spell on him. Rivera did not attend a formal school until he was eight; he was an excellent student but could not seem to abandon his penchant for high jinks. Even before he finished elementary school, he began attending night classes at the San Carlos School of Fine Arts. He was by far the youngest student there—he'd lied about his age in order to qualify for admission—yet after only two years he won second prize in the school's drawing competition. He received a scholarship and began taking regular daytime classes. Rivera found several instructors there who encouraged his love of nature and of Indian art. Still, he later wrote that his most influential "teacher" was José Guadalupe Posada, who owned a small printing shop where he produced sheets of poems and songs for local musicians and singers. Posada illustrated these by engraving traditional Mexican Indian designs on the metal printing plates. The designs enchanted Rivera, and he spent hours in Posada's shop discussing art and other matters.

Rivera soon tired of the traditional European styles that he studied in art school. At age 16 he left school and began traveling around Mexico, drawing and painting and trying to earn enough money to travel to Europe. He had not yet achieved fame, but he was already large in stature; even in his late teens he was tremendous—about 300 pounds and six feet tall. During these years, Rivera's involvement in his country's political and social problems deepened. Poverty was rampant, and no laws existed to protect laborers. Near the end of 1906, a band of workers organized a march to the president's palace to ask for help. The president ordered the army to open fire on the demonstrators, and many men, women, and children were killed or injured. The incident—which initiated a turbulent period in Mexican politics—was indelibly stamped on the minds of socially concerned Mexicans like Rivera.

The artist was ultimately able to go to Europe and stayed there from 1907 to 1921. He began his journey in Spain, where he studied the work of the master painters **Diego Velazquez, El Greco,** and **Francisco Goya** (see entries). He then settled in Paris, remaining there until 1921, though he did traverse much of Europe. Rivera found himself in the center of the Parisian art world; his friends were the great artists of the day: painters **Pablo Picasso** (see entry), Georges Braque, Amedeo Modigliani, and many others. He painted a number of works in the style of **cubism,** using Mexican ideas and themes.

Embraces communist ideals

Rivera's relationships with women were stormy throughout his life. Several such attachments were lengthy ones, the first in Paris, with a Russian painter named Angeline Belloff. Belloff's stories of Russia and its politics captured Rivera's imagination. He was familiar with the writings and philosophy of communism, and when the Bolshevik Revolution erupted in Russia in 1917, Rivera fervently, if a bit naively, hoped that the ideals of communism—workers' rights and a more equitable distribution of wealth—would be put into practice. Rivera and Belloff lived together for roughly a decade and had a son, Diego Rivera, Jr., who was born in 1916; the boy died when he was two years old.

While in Europe Rivera visited Mexico several times and was always troubled by the political strife there. The government changed constantly, and there was little peace or prosperity. Around 1920 Rivera decided to return to the country of his birth, intending to produce art for all of the people, not just rich collectors. His last months in Europe were spent studying **frescoes** in Italy, among them the Sistine Chapel in Rome, painted by the great Renaissance master **Michelangelo** (see entry). Rivera became convinced that wall frescoes, painted on freshly spread plaster with water-based pigments, would be an ideal medium for a people's art; such works would be accessible to everyone, not just to those who could afford to visit museums or buy artwork.

During the 1920s Rivera gained considerable recognition. He painted **murals** for several public buildings, the first at the auditorium of the University of Mexico's National Preparatory School. While working there he met and married a young Mexican woman, Guadalupe Marín. They were married for five years and had two daughters. Rivera often used Marín as a model. Up to this time, most of Rivera's work echoed European tradition. But during the early 1920s, through travel in the provinces of Mexico, he arrived at an even greater appreciation for the cultural heritage of the Mexican people, elements of which surfaced with increasing frequency in his work.

Cements reputation with murals

As the decade progressed, Rivera was chiefly occupied with his murals and various union and political activities. Murals from this period cover walls at the Ministry of Public Education and the Palacio Nacional, the capitol building, in Mexico City, and at the Agricultural College at Chapingo. They are massive paintings, as long as city blocks, and took years to complete. Assistants would prepare a section of wall at night, and Rivera would arrive at dawn to do the actual painting, working until sunset. The process of frescoing requires quick and precise work because the plaster dries in less than 12 hours and afterward won't absorb paint properly.

The subjects of Rivera's murals were often controversial; he did not portray traditional scenes of gods and heroes, great battles, or religious narratives. Instead, he strove to present the Mexican people—farmers, miners, weavers, families, children—and events like weddings and holidays. His murals at the Agricultural College at Chapingo demonstrate his faith in communist ideals, with titles like *Good Government, Dividing the Land,* and *Formation of Revolutionary Leadership.* The *History of Mexico* murals at the Palacio Nacional are the most extensive story of a country ever painted. Rivera particularly emphasized

the grand civilizations of Mexico before its conquest by Europeans, the cruelties of the ruling Spanish, and the struggle for independence. These were not the subjects government officials had expected.

In fact, there were calls for these radical works to be destroyed, but in the end, many art lovers and critics from around the world—the very people Rivera had snubbed as elitists—prevailed on the Mexican government to preserve the murals. These controversies brought Rivera international recognition. Mexico became the center of a mural revival, with Rivera in the lead; numerous artists came to study with him and learn the fresco technique. Some—including David Alfaro Siqueiros and José Clemente Orozco—went on to fame themselves. The popularity of his work led to commissions for Rivera in the United States during the 1930s.

Also that decade, Rivera met and married a young artist and fellow communist, **Frida Kahlo** (see entry). Kahlo became Rivera's constant companion and supporter until her death in

1954. Although their relationship was sometimes rocky, they worked closely and were active in politics together for 25 years. Shortly after their marriage, they made their first trip to the United States, to paint a mural for the Pacific Stock Exchange building in San Francisco. Rivera and Kahlo were treated like celebrities, but, as was becoming the norm, criticism and controversy were stirred up by the social and political aspects of the finished fresco; a similar brouhaha attended a small mural Rivera did for the California School for the Fine Arts.

Detroit frescoes continue pattern of controversy

Rivera's next commission became the most important work of his career. In 1932 he agreed to paint a series of frescoes for the courtyard of the Detroit Institute of Arts detailing the history of Detroit and the growth of industry. The *Detroit Industry* frescoes illuminate the power and beauty of machinery and the strength and nobility of workers. Rivera and Kahlo spent over a month in Detroit before starting the work; they toured factories, watched automobiles and other machinery being constructed, and talked to workers. The colorful, dynamic frescoes cover a broad range of topics, from the origins of human life, to the development of agriculture, to the growth of the automotive and aviation industries. The murals depict such notable figures as automotive magnate Henry Ford, inventor Thomas Edison, and Rivera himself. The style of these works exhibits the influences of the many schools Rivera had seen and studied: Aztec, cubist, Italian **Renaissance,** and Mexican folk art.

Like his other works, these frescoes caused an uproar. Some observers called them inappropriate for an art museum, sacrilegious, and even pornographic. Once again the international art world intervened to save the frescoes from destruction. Rivera's next commissioned work, however, would not be so blessed.

With his fame at its height, Rivera was asked by the powerful and wealthy Rockefeller family to paint a mural at Rockefeller Center in New York City. The sketches for the work were approved ahead of time, but apparently the Rockefellers did not anticipate the power of Rivera's imagery and his un-

Social Realism in the United States

The first three decades of the twentieth century saw enormous experimentation in art in the United States and around the world. The **avant-garde**—those on the cutting edge of artistic creation and theory—exercised a huge influence on the mainstream. But by the 1920s some artists had begun to reject the extremes of the avant-garde; they reasoned that art should be meaningful to everyone, not exclusively to those who could understand complex ideas and philosophies. Moving away from what they considered the rarefied and elitist terms of avant-garde thought, they emphasized instead art's capacity to inform and inspire. Rather than the riddles of dreams, they focused on society and political change. Thus began the social realism movement, which flourished in the 1930s.

The principle followers of social realism came from many different backgrounds and painted in a variety of styles. Their endeavors were united by a common desire for social change and the use of very real subject matter in their art. They were primarily concerned with poverty, especially during the Great Depression of the 1930s, and with racial equality, the problems of workers and labor unions, and with the stresses of urban and industrial life in modern times. Sometimes their paintings were observations of urban ghetto life, as in the work of **Jacob Lawrence** (see entry). Often they depicted an actual event, such as

canny ability to portray the contrasts between rich and poor; nor did they seem to grasp his faith in communism as the salvation of workers. The final straw came when Rivera included the face of Russian Communist leader Vladimir Ilich Lenin in the mural. Months of scandal, publicity, and bitter feelings followed, with armed guards surrounding the murals, workers picketing the site, and charges of censorship echoing in the press. Fortunately, one of Rivera's assistants managed to photograph the mural secretly before it was destroyed in 1934.

Throughout the 1930s and 1940s Rivera and Kahlo continued to paint, teach, and remain active in communist and workers' causes. Rivera executed a few projects in Mexico and the United States and painted various portraits and other works, many in a style related to **surrealism.** He also assembled a collection

Ben Shahn's series of paintings portraying the famous trial of accused murderers Sacco and Vanzetti. Philip Evergood's 1937 painting *American Tragedy* presents Chicago police clashing with a group of steelworkers during a protest march.

Despite social realism's name, it is not strictly a realistic style; purely imitative or naturalistic representation is usually less important than the artist's message. Many social realists used exaggerated features and distorted space for effect. Some used bright colors for emotional impact, while others employed a "primitive" style, with dark outlines and geometric shapes. Social realists at times tried to achieve a photographic clarity to better indicate the realness of their subjects. Elements of the dream-like style of surrealism were periodically utilized in social realism to illustrate the alienation of contemporary life. Rivera's work, particularly his murals in New York City, San Francisco, and Detroit, exerted a vast influence on American artists. Mural and wall art achieved unprecedented popularity in the 1930s, especially in government-sponsored projects in public buildings. Some of these murals remain in—and on—post offices and court buildings from the period.

Social realism did not die out in the 1930s. Many artists in the decades that followed retained a passionate belief that art must serve truth and function as a force for social change and justice.

of ancient stone and clay idols and statues—more than 60,000—for which he built a museum south of Mexico City called Anahuacalli; it became the property of the Mexican people after Rivera's death.

In 1949 a huge exhibit of Rivera's work opened in Mexico City, with more than a thousand of his creations gathered from around the world. The president of Mexico declared Rivera "a national treasure." The painter had not finished generating art or controversy, but both his health and Frida Kahlo's deteriorated throughout the late 1940s and into the 1950s. Kahlo died in 1954; Rivera worked continuously until his death in 1957 at the age of 70.

In the years since Rivera's death, his work has been the subject of even greater acclaim, while the images he employed and

his ideas about the public nature of art have gained increasing acceptance. He was one of the first artists to promote the native culture and art of Mexico, helping to stimulate the serious examination and revaluation of folk art. At the same time, his art celebrated the progress of technology and industry in the modern era. He spurred many of his admirers to celebrate their own artistic heritage and to use their art in pursuit of social justice.

Masterworks

Paintings

1915	*Zapatista Landscape— The Guerrilla*
1939	*Girl with Mask*
1947	*Peasants*
1952	*The Nightmare of War and the Dream of Peace*
1956	*The Ice Breakers*

Frescoes

1923-28	Ministry of Public Education, Mexico City
1924-27	Agricultural School, Chapingo, Mexico
1928-29	Palacio Nacional, *History of Mexico*
1932-33	Detroit Institute of Arts, *Detroit Industry*
	Rockefeller Center, New York, *Man at the Crossroads* (destroyed)

◀ *Rivera at work on the* **Man at the Crossroads** *fresco at Rockefeller Center in New York City, May 10, 1933; the controversial image of Lenin is at right. Reproduced by permission of AP/Wide World Photos.*

Auguste Rodin

Born November 12, 1840
Paris, France

Died November 17, 1917
Meudon, France

"I see all the truth, not only that of the outside. I reproduce the spirit."

▲ *Portrait: Reproduced by permission of The Bettmann Archive.*

The sculptor Auguste Rodin rebelled against the traditions of classicism he felt were suffocating his medium, opting instead for realism and emotional directness. His work—dedicated to evoking the inner states of his subjects—stirred tremendous controversy. Ultimately, however, he emerged as the most influential sculptor of the post-Renaissance era.

Rodin's parents, Jean-Baptiste and Marie Cheffer Rodin, came to Paris from the countryside in the 1830s; Jean-Baptiste Rodin served as a clerk with the police department and later worked as a prison inspector. The devoutly religious Rodins sent Auguste and his sister Maria to Catholic school. But the boy learned little there, spending most of his time drawing. He often copied pictures from the illustrated newspapers that the family's grocer used as wrapping paper. When he was ten his parents enrolled the budding artist in his uncle's school in Beauvais, a city north of Paris. He hated it there and returned home a few years later. Historians suspect that Rodin's trouble in school may have stemmed in part from the fact that he was severely near-sighted and never had his vision corrected with glasses. This may also explain part of sculpture's appeal for him, since in that form he could rely a great deal on his hands rather than entirely on his eyes.

Rodin's father allowed the 14-year-old Auguste to enroll in a Paris vocational school to study commercial art and decoration. Here the students spent much of their time copying the work of eighteenth-century decorators and ornamental painters. Fortunately for Rodin, one teacher had some new ideas about teaching art and encouraged in the students an unusual freedom, despite the disapproval of other teachers. This experience inspired Rodin to continue his studies. He spent many hours sketching statues in the Louvre, France's national museum, and attended lectures at a university to learn about literature and poetry.

Thrice denied admission to School of Fine Arts

Despite his success at art school, Rodin was denied three times when he applied for admission to the celebrated School of Fine Arts in Paris. He supported himself by working for commercial designers, assisting them in such tasks as mixing plaster and smoothing mold marks out of plaster casts. In his own studio Rodin produced statues of nymphs, cupids, and other figures in the neo-classical style that predominated during the period.

The death of Auguste's sister, Maria, when he was 22—she was two years his senior—affected him greatly. For a while he thought of becoming a monk, but the priest he consulted at a monastery knew of his talent and advised him to continue with his art. He set up his studio in an unheated stable in Paris. Although he continued to model statuary in the popular mode, he also worked on his own style.

Rodin's best known work from this time, about 1864, is *Man with the Broken Nose.* His model was a local man who did odd jobs; Rodin was fascinated by the shape of the man's head, his twisted nose, and the tragic but noble expression on his face. When Rodin entered the piece in a show run by the official government **Salon,** the judges were shocked by its rough, lifelike demeanor. The approved style of the day was based on the physical perfection and impassive expressions of the graceful personages of Greek and Roman mythology. Against such a standard, Rodin's rough-hewn *Man* was deemed an abomination; the judges rejected it. The sculptor later said, "It was the first good piece of modeling I ever did." This style became his trademark. He endured criticism for it throughout his career but found it most appropriate for the expression of his ideas.

Around the time he wrought *Man with the Broken Nose,* Rodin met a young seamstress named Rose Beuret. She enjoyed modeling for him and eventually became his mistress, housekeeper, and studio helper. Their son was born in 1866. Although Rodin and his friends often mistreated Rose because of her relative lack of education and sophistication, she never abandoned the artist; they were together for close to 50 years. When they were both in their seventies, Rodin finally married his faithful companion. She died two weeks later.

During the 1860s the young couple led a happy though poor life in Paris. Rodin was hired as an assistant in the studio of Albert-Ernest Carrier-Belleuse, one of France's most reputable sculptors. He immediately recognized Rodin's talent and allowed him more freedom in working on his sculptures than was allowed the other assistants. In his spare time Rodin modeled numerous busts of Rose, the most famous being *Young Woman in Flowered Hat.*

During the war between France and Prussia in the early 1870s, Rodin served in the National Guard; hard economic times followed the war. Carrier-Belleuse was working on a large commission in Belgium and asked his talented young charge to join him. Rodin stayed there for several years, working with his mentor and other sculptors, and was eventually able to send some money to Rose in Paris. In 1875 he traveled to Italy and spent three months studying the sculpture of ancient Greece and Rome and of the Italian **Renaissance,** especially the work of **Michelangelo** (see entry).

Absorbs energy and emotion of Michelangelo's work

The energy and emotion Rodin saw in Michelangelo's work had a deep effect on him. Returning to Paris the next year, Rodin felt an even greater impatience for the neoclassical statuary at the Salon exhibits and elsewhere—smoothly inexpressive goddesses and young athletes that slavishly copied the superior Athenian and Roman originals. He was not alone in his feeling; painting was undergoing the stirrings of what would become a stylistic revolution. **Impressionism** had attracted considerable interest, and Rodin hoped to inject a similar spirit and energy into sculpture.

Soon after his return from Italy, Rodin hired a male model who reminded him of one of Michelangelo's figures. He sculpted him in a standing position, his head thrown back, one hand resting on his head. Rodin caused a sensation in the Belgian capital of Brussels when he exhibited the standing figure in 1877. Many viewers found it too lifelike to be a sculpture and accused Rodin of constructing it from casts of the model's body. Rodin was angered and hurt by these accusations. He defended his work, and other artists rallied to support him. Eventually he was vindicated: the Belgian government bought a cast of the work and placed it in a public garden. After this, Rodin's works were widely sought after, though they continued to provoke controversy.

In 1880 the French Minister of Fine Arts commissioned Rodin to design a doorway for a planned Decorative Arts Museum; this became the greatest project of the artist's life. He worked on it for 37 years, creating nearly 200 figures for the doorway that he called *The Gates of Hell*. Ultimately, though, it would be left unfinished. Many of Rodin's most renowned sculptures are individual figures taken from the doorway, which presents themes from Dante's *Inferno* and the Bible—scenes inspired by Michelangelo's Sistine Chapel frescoes—medieval stories of hell, and contemporary French writing. The tortured, reaching, crawling, embracing figures display an astonishing spectrum of human emotion.

Sculpts *The Thinker*

The most easily recognized figure from the *Gates of Hell* is *The Thinker*. This seated figure of a man with his chin resting on his hand has become not only one of the world's foremost art treasures but a virtual symbol of modern sculpture. Of his figure Rodin wrote, "He thinks not only with his brain, but with every muscle of his arms, back and legs, with his clenched fist and gripping toes."

Rodin saw marked success through the 1880s and 1890s. He maintained several studios with large staffs of assistants. Each studio tackled different projects commissioned by governments and private interests. Perhaps the best known of these is his monument for the city of Calais, France, called *The Burghers of Calais*. It depicts six fourteenth-century town leaders who became heroes for offering themselves as hostages to the King of England in order to save Calais. Rather than depicting these men in traditional heroic poses, Rodin sculpted each figure to best convey a range of feelings. Once again the public, not to mention the town committee of Calais, were shocked by the rough modeling of the subjects and the intensely human emotions evident in their faces. The city refused to place the monument in front of the town hall and would not pay Rodin to have the statue cast in bronze. Despite this rejection, the sculptor considered

The Burghers of Calais, 1886. Bronze, 82½" x 95" x 78". Rodin Museum, Paris. Reproduced by permission of Foto Marburg/Art Resource, NY.

Auguste Rodin

How Is Sculpture Made?

Sculpture, unlike painting, occupies a three-dimensional space. Thus the viewer's experience of a work of sculpture is very different from that of a painting: one can view a statue from various angles and observe new details from each vantage point. At times sculpted figures appear lifelike enough to confuse onlookers—like the twentieth-century creations of George Segal—while mimes of sufficient skill can even pose as statues. Sculpture often has more varied textures than other media, and if one is lucky, such pieces can be appreciated with the fingers as well as the eyes. Indeed, many museums permit blind visitors to touch all but the most fragile sculpture. By the early twentieth century, sculpture even began to move.

Before the twentieth century, almost all sculpture was made of stone, wood, clay, or metal. Modern artists have incorporated such new materials as plastic, aluminum, steel, styrofoam, and even light bulbs, expanding both the definition and the vocabulary of the medium.

Sculptors have shaped traditional materials in three ways. Wood and stone are carved using special tools designed for chipping and smoothing. Artists of the past, such as Michelangelo, utilized a hammer and chisel for such tasks; today, some artists use electric drills. The sculptor cuts away the unwanted material to form the shapes desired and then often smooths or polishes the surface. The artist must have a mental picture of the finished product before beginning to carve. The size of the sculpture is limited by the size of the tree trunk or piece of stone with which he or she begins.

Artists also produce sculpture by modeling with clay or wax. These materials are pliable and can thus be molded into almost any shape. They are not particularly sturdy, however, and usually dry out and crack over time. Yet because they enable artists to easily add and remove pieces—virtually impossible with wood or stone—these softer materials provide greater flexibility. For large clay sculptures, sculptors often use an "armature," or supporting skeleton made of wood or wire, building up clay on top of it.

To make these works more durable, several techniques have been developed. Clay can be fired in an oven called a kiln and sometimes glazed, as is the case with much of pottery. This increases its durability, but such pieces remain fragile.

The strongest sculpture comes from metal casting, a complicated and expensive process developed by ancient Greek and

The Burghers his most successful monument. It eventually was cast, but almost 40 years passed before it was installed in front of the town hall; by then Rodin had been dead for seven years.

Chinese artists. In the most common form of casting, known as the "lost wax" technique, the artist makes a mold of wax or plaster around a clay prototype. Molten metal, often bronze, is poured into the mold, which melts the wax or plaster to leave a metal representation of the outer surface of the clay. After the metal hardens, the mold is removed and the artist can smooth away any uneven areas. In modern times a technique using sand instead of wax was developed, allowing several casts to be made from the same mold. Traditional sculpture dictates that rough spots be removed from the clay surface and the metal cast smoothed and polished. Auguste Rodin was the first artist to leave lumps of clay showing in order to create an effect; he often left the rough surface of the metal and even the mold marks. Viewers at the time thought Rodin's works were unfinished. He felt the roughness invested his work with greater reality and feeling.

Modern artists have greatly expanded the boundaries of sculpture. Industry developed new materials like steel tubes and sheet metal; as a result, a whole new kind of sculpture or construction could be made. Tubes of varying thickness could be creatively assembled, shapes could be cut from metal or designs painted on it, wires might form latticework—a world of post-industrial art emerged. Artists could use welding, or the melting together of metal parts, to achieve greater flexibility and scope in their sculptures.

A revolution in sculpture took place beginning around 1910 as artists began to experiment with these new means. Among the principles they embraced was motion. As **Alexander Calder** (see entry) and other artists demonstrated, sculpture would no longer necessarily represent a moment frozen in time. With hinges, weights, motors, or just the wind, a sculpture could define and change the space around it. Sculpture in motion came to be called **kinetic art.**

These new techniques made artists question why a sculpture needed to be made of a single material. Picasso and the other cubists responded by creating **collages,** gluing objects onto their paintings. Contemporary sculptors combine a wide variety of materials—often called "found objects"—in both abstract and more representational works. To be sure, today's sculptors have a far broader palette of materials and techniques from which to choose than had their predecessors. What hasn't changed, however, is the need to use the imagination to transform lifeless matter into creations that inspire, infuriate, move on their own, and all but breathe.

Although Rodin endured substantial criticism and at times outright condemnation, and despite countless rejections of his works, he has come to be regarded as one of the greatest sculp-

Masterworks

1876	*The Age of Bronze*
1877	*Walking Man*
1877	*St. John the Baptist Preaching*
1880-1917	*The Gates of Hell* (unfinished)
1880	*The Thinker* (from *The Gates of Hell*)
1886	*The Burghers of Calais*
1897	*Balzac*

tors of the human figure. In his later years he became fascinated with the female form and struggled to capture the movement and spirit of dancers in his sculpture and drawing. Beyond his many enduring works, his other crucial success lay in the concepts and techniques he handed down to the generations that followed him. Aspiring artists like French painter **Henri Matisse,** Spanish painter **Pablo Picasso,** and Romanian sculptor **Constantin Brancusi** (see entries) came to study with him, experimenting with his ideas or rejecting them to find their own. Although Rodin's roots were firmly in the past, his boldly emotional work helped open the door for future innovations. When he died in 1917, the figure of *The Thinker* was installed as the headstone of his grave to underline the importance of the constant search for new ideas in artistic pursuit.

Peter Paul Rubens

Born June 28, 1577
Siegen, Westphalia (Germany)
Died May 30, 1640
Antwerp, Flanders (Belgium)

The genius of seventeenth-century Flemish painter Peter Paul Rubens lies in his combination of the energetic, realistic styles then prevalent in Northern Europe and the beauty and light of the Italian **Renaissance.** In this synthesis he served as artistic diplomat, much as he served as an actual diplomat to several European nations. The success Rubens enjoyed in his many endeavors is reflected in the joy and verve of his work. Indeed, during his lifetime he was perhaps the most popular painter in all of Europe. His subjects included scenes from religion, classical mythology, history, as well as everyday life. This variety, coupled with his lively style, have ensured his place as one of the best-loved painters in the history of art.

The Rubens family came from Antwerp, a bustling city in Flanders, the area of Europe north of France now known as Belgium. At the time Rubens and his older brother were born the family was living in exile in Westphalia (Germany), victims of religious persecution. Much of Europe at this time was expe-

"His unrivaled gifts in arranging large colourful compositions and in infusing them with buoyant energy secured a fame and success for Rubens such as no painter had enjoyed before."

E. H. Gombrich

| Peter Paul Rubens

riencing major conflict between Catholics and Protestants. Rubens and his brother were well educated by their father. By the time he was 13, Rubens spoke four languages and later learned several others. He was always interested in drawing and spent many hours copying pictures from books.

Rubens and his family returned to Antwerp after his father died. His family encouraged him to pursue law, but he nonetheless chose to become an artist. He served as an apprentice, or assistant, to several painters during his teenage years. The last of his teachers urged Rubens to go to Italy to study. He finally went in May 1600, when he was 22 years old.

In Venice Rubens beheld the work of Italian painters including **Titian,** Veronese, and Tintoretto. In Rome he saw the masterpieces of Raphael and **Michelangelo** (see entries). He also took note of the dramatic lighting employed by a young painter of the time named Caravaggio. Rubens's style was greatly affected by the beautiful color, dramatic composition, and use of light in these works.

Court painter and diplomat

From 1602 to 1608 Rubens was court painter to the Duke of Mantua, a city in Italy. The duke's court was exceptionally wealthy and cultured; among his fine possessions was a large collection of artworks and a menagerie of exotic animals, including tigers and crocodiles. His entourage numbered scientists, artists, actors, and musicians. Rubens held two positions in Mantua. He produced paintings, many of them copies of older works. And because of his charm and intelligence, he was also sent on diplomatic missions as the duke's representative. His first such outing was to Spain in 1603; he spent nearly a year there.

During his years in Italy, Rubens absorbed many of the concepts of Italian painting, as well as the mythology, sculpture, and architecture of the country. It is not surprising that many of his paintings from this period resemble those of the various Italian artists he studied. Indeed, he had yet to develop a personal style.

Rubens was forced to hurriedly leave Italy and return to Antwerp in 1608 when news reached him that his mother was ill. But he was too late to see her before she died. After mourning his mother and hanging one of his finest paintings in the church where she was buried, Rubens made plans to return to Italy. Before he could go, though, the Flemish government appointed him court painter—news of his talents in art and diplomacy having spread from Italy. Rubens agreed to stay in Flanders. Within a short time he was busy with many commissions.

The next year, 1609, Rubens married a young woman, Isabella Brandt. One of his favorite paintings is a portrait of himself and Isabella shortly after their marriage. It depicts them seated in a garden, holding hands and dressed in festive, opulent clothing full of ruffles and lace. The scene has a warm and happy feeling to it. With the income from his many commissions, he built a large home, with studios and rooms for his apprentices. Rubens and his wife had three children, two boys and a girl. The painter's daughter, however, died when she was quite young.

The Golden Age.
Reproduced by permission of The Bettmann Archive.

Combined northern realism with Italian Renaissance

During the next few years, Rubens's career and style continued to develop. He began to meld the ideas he encountered in Italy with the typical northern styles of painting he had learned as a youth. The result was a new mode that emphasized rich light and warm color and also displayed the Flemish attempt to represent the natural world. Rubens's reputations spread like wildfire and soon he began to receive commissions from all over Europe. He painted many church altarpieces, portraits of wealthy people, narratives from history and mythology, and even hunting scenes. The output from his studio was enormous.

Rubens was able to meet the fierce demand for his work by organizing his studio almost like a factory production line. He completed early sketches and models for his various works, then assistants and students would enlarge the ideas onto canvas and add color. Rubens would refine the color application and attend to finishing details. He often charged his patrons more if he personally spent a lot of time on the work. Because of this system, there has been some confusion over the years as to just how much of each work can actually be attributed to Rubens; in museums it is not uncommon to see a painting identified as "School of Rubens," meaning that it came from his workshop but Rubens himself may not have painted it. As Rubens became internationally renowned, young artists flocked to Antwerp hoping to work under the great master. Several of his students became acclaimed painters themselves, among them Anthony Van Dyck and Jacob Jordaens.

The 1620s marked the height of Rubens's career both as an artist and a diplomat. He painted numerous series of large paintings portraying historical events. The most celebrated of these is a series of 21 paintings titled *The Life of Marie de Medici,* the queen of France. Rubens prepared sketches for these paintings in Paris, and they were finished in his workshop. They have been called his greatest achievement. By then his style had developed into what is termed **baroque** art, characterized by energetic movement, rich color, and dramatic light. Sometimes the

Peter Paul Rubens   400

themes captured seem to burst out of the frame. Typical elements of the style include swirling draperies and clouds, unusual **perspectives,** and careful attention to details like curls, jewelry, and skin texture. Rubens's work in particular is known for its representation of the human form. The physique of men is usually portrayed as strong and muscular; women often are very plump, with soft, pink skin. This look is still known today as "Rubenesque."

Befriended Spanish master Velazquez

In 1626 Rubens's wife, Isabella, died. Rubens began to accept frequent diplomatic missions from the Flemish court. He was sent to Spain in 1628. There he painted portraits of King Philip IV and the royal family. A much-repeated story from this era relates how as Rubens was painting one day, a courtier came by and remarked, "So the ambassador amuses himself with paint-

Peter Paul Rubens

Masterworks

1609	*The Artist and Isabella Brandt*
1610	*The Raising of the Cross*
1623	*Maria de Medici, Queen of France, Landing in Marseilles*
1625	*Adoration of the Magi*
1630	*Allegory on the Blessings of Peace*
1632	*The Judgment of Paris*
	The Feast of Venus
1636	*Landscape with the Chateau of Steen*
1639	*Self-Portrait*

ing?" Rubens replied, "Perhaps it is the painter who amuses himself with diplomacy." This courtier was the king's chief painter, **Diego Velazquez** (see entry). The two artists became friends and spent much time together discussing art and studying the king's collection of paintings by Titian. It was Rubens who persuaded King Philip to send Velazquez to study art in Italy.

Another important mission of the 1620s was Rubens's trip to England. He stayed there for nine months conducting peace negotiations. He also managed to pursue his artwork there, producing a much-lauded painted ceiling for a royal banqueting hall. In fact, King Charles I admired Rubens so much that he granted him a knighthood, bestowing on him the title Sir Rubens. Later, the King of Spain also knighted Rubens, making him the only painter so honored by both monarchs.

In 1630, his workshop still busy, Rubens married for the second time. His new wife, Helena Fourment, was just 19 years old. She served as his inspiration for many portraits and scenes from mythology. They had five children. Rubens's work of the 1630s reached even greater sophistication as his technique was perfected. He began using softer colors and a more relaxed approach to his various themes. But during these years Rubens also developed gout, a painful disease that causes swelling in the joints. He sometimes experienced difficulty handling his paintbrushes, but he continued to accept commissions, counting on his assistants to complete them. He even let some of them sign their names to his works during these years. In 1635 Rubens bought a large estate in the country and spent much of his time there painting landscapes. They have been described as "glowing" and "joyous." One writer commented, "These works alone would ensure his fame ... [even] if no other works survived." His landscapes especially were influential to later artists.

In a self-portrait painted shortly before his death, Rubens pictured himself as an elegant gentleman, sporting a black velvet cloak and the jeweled sword presented to him by King Charles. His gout-crippled hand is covered with a glove. The work amply conveys the honor, prosperity, and intelligence that marked Rubens's life and work. At the time of his death his popularity was unparalleled. And more than 300 years later, artists and art lovers the world over continue to admire and draw inspiration from his gifts.

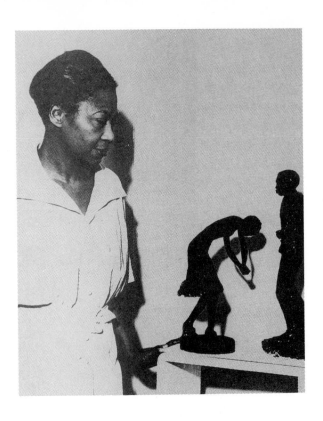

Augusta Savage

Born February 29, 1892
Green Cove Springs, Florida
Died March 27, 1962
New York, New York

*"How am I
to compete with
other American
artists if I am not to
be given the same
opportunity?"*

▲ *Portrait: Schomburg
Center for Research in
Black Culture, The New
York Public Library.*

Despite a lifetime spent combatting the effects of racism and sexism, Augusta Savage's accomplishments were many. She was a talented sculptor, an admired teacher, and a fighter for the rights of African Americans. Her circumstances were never easy, though she was afforded financial help and artistic encouragement from several sources. In addition to her achievements in sculpture, she contributed to the history of art in America by helping to launch the careers of a number of other artists during the 1930s and 1940s.

The topsoil in the area where Augusta Christine Fells (later Savage) grew up in Florida was made of red clay, and the major industry there was brick making. It was in her own backyard that Savage learned to model with clay. Her family was very poor. She and her 13 brothers and sisters had no toys. But Savage found that she could amuse herself and others by making clay ducks, pigs, and other animals. She loved working the clay so much that she sometimes missed school to visit the town's clay pit. Savage's father was a minister, a deeply religious and very strict man. He did not approve of his daughter making images of "God's creatures" out of clay.

When Savage was about 15, her family moved to West Palm Beach, Florida. Their life improved greatly there. The principal of Savage's new school discovered her modeling talents and offered her a dollar a day to teach clay modeling classes. During this time Savage married John T. Moore and the couple had a daughter, born in 1908. Moore died a few years later. Savage continued to live with her parents. She was married again around 1915, to James Savage, a carpenter. They were divorced in 1921.

Wowed county fair with clay animals

During this period Savage attended a state teacher's school (now Florida A & M University) for one year in Tallahassee, Florida. To earn money she convinced the superintendent of the local county fair, George Currie, to let her set up a booth to sell her animal sculptures. Fair officials at first objected to a black woman having her own booth, but they finally agreed. Savage's animals were very popular and she made about $150, more money than she'd ever had. Fair officials also awarded her a $25 prize for the most original exhibit.

Currie believed that Savage had a lot of talent. He encouraged her to go to New York and gave her a letter of introduction to a sculptor he knew in the city. Savage arrived in New York in 1921 with less than five dollars. But Currie's friend arranged for her to take art classes at a tuition-free school called the Cooper Union. She landed a job as an apartment caretaker to cover living expenses. Three months later, though, she lost her job and soon found herself penniless. Recognizing her talent, the Cooper Union Advisory Board voted to supply funds to meet Savage's living expenses. This was the first time the school sponsored a student.

In New York Savage became interested in African art and spent a lot of time at the public library reading and doing research. She befriended the librarian there. When the librarian found out about Savage's dire financial straits, she arranged for the library to hire Savage to sculpt a bust of the famous African American thinker and writer W. E. B. Du Bois. This was Savage's first commission; several others followed, including one of another black leader, Marcus Garvey. These works earned Savage considerable recognition among the important figures of the Harlem Renaissance. Harlem was the predominantly African American neighborhood of New York. During the 1920s and 1930s this community was experiencing a particularly active and exciting period of creativity in the arts.

Stung by racism

In 1923 Savage's career received a setback when she encountered a fierce incident of racial prejudice. The French government was offering scholarships to 100 American women to study at a summer art school in Paris. Savage applied for the $500 scholarship and gathered pledges from friends and acquaintances to pay for her travel and other expenses. Her application was returned when the committee learned she was of African descent. Savage was disappointed and outraged. She decided to fight the rejection and gathered many prominent people behind her. Her cause garnered considerable publicity. In an article in the *New York World,* Savage explained that she was not raising a fuss just for herself. "Other and better colored students might wish to apply sometime.... I don't like to see them establish a precedent." Still, Savage felt personally stung. "My brother was good enough to be ... [in a] regiment that saw service in France during the war, but it seems his sister is not good enough to be a guest of the country for which he fought.... How am I to compete with other American artists if I am not to be given the same opportunity?"

This experience inspired Savage to become active in the political and social issues concerning African Americans. Eventually, some factions of the art world began to consider her a "troublemaker"; a few historians have even surmised that she was purposely excluded from exhibits and galleries because of the flap over the scholarship. But through the efforts of W. E. B. Du Bois, Savage was awarded a scholarship in 1925 to study in Italy. She desperately longed to go, knowing that European study would refine her sculpting techniques. But the little money she was earning working in a laundry was needed to feed her family, who had left Florida to join her in New York. This time she was not able to raise money from those who had supported her in the past.

In the meantime, Savage continued to develop her style. She produced many small clay figures of people around the city. One became especially popular and is considered among her best works. It is the head of a boy, with his hat turned at a jaunty angle and a streetwise expression on his face. Savage called this piece *Gamin*. When it was featured on the cover of a magazine, it caught the eye of the head of the National Urban League. He asked the Julius Rosenwald Fund, a philanthropic organization established by the founder of the department store Sears Roebuck, to award Savage a scholarship. The grant afforded her enough money to cover living and travel expenses for two years. When her scholarship awards were announced, other groups raised money for her as well, including African American women's groups and teachers at her former school, Florida A & M. They understood the discrimination she had suffered at the hands of the French scholarship board and wished to support her.

Nurtured careers of budding artists

Savage's dream to study in Europe finally came true. In 1930 and 1931 she studied sculpture in Paris and traveled throughout the Continent. Her works were shown in numerous exhibitions and won awards from two. Moreover, an African figure she designed was selected to adorn a medal for an important French exposition. Savage continued sculpting on her return to New York in 1931. The Great Depression was making life very hard then, especially for African Americans. Nonetheless, the early 1930s were a very busy time for Savage; they found her creating portraits of many prominent African Americans, including abolitionist Frederick Douglass, poet James Weldon Johnson, composer W. C. Handy, and others. It was also during this period that she founded the Savage Studio of Arts and Crafts in Harlem, where she taught many classes, several for children. This studio became the focus of her career in the 1930s. She encountered many talented young people in Harlem and was instrumental in starting their careers. Her students described Savage as a very inspirational teacher, while also acknowledging that she could be very stern and demanding. **Jacob Lawrence** (see entry), Gwendolyn Knight, and Norman Lewis are just three who benefited from Savage's help and encouragement.

As the 1930s continued, Savage spent less and less time on her own artworks and more on teaching and community activities. In 1937 she was appointed the first director of the Harlem Community Art Center, where she organized classes in art, education, and recreation. She also became an important figure in the government-sponsored programs of the Works Progress Administration, which were designed to help artists financially during the Depression. In 1939 Savage opened the Salon of Contemporary Negro Art, a gallery specializing in the art of African Americans. Despite her growing prominence in the community, it closed after a few years.

The last major commission Savage received came when she was one of four women, and the only African American, asked to create sculptures for the 1939 New York World's Fair. She took as inspiration a line from a song known as the "Negro National Anthem." Called *Lift Every Voice and Sing,* the huge sculpture bore the shape of a harp, each string a figure of a child with his or her mouth open in song. The piece became one of the most popular attractions at the fair. Nonetheless, the plaster cast displayed there was never rendered in stone or metal. It was destroyed after the event. This was the fate of many of Savage's works as her meager funds rarely enabled her to permanently cast them. Only a few of her many creations survive.

Around 1940 Savage moved to a farm in upstate New York; she cut all ties to friends and the art world. She produced few works, preferring to spend her hours laboring on the farm or teaching an occasional art class for local children. Perhaps the years of financial and artistic struggle, much of it the result of racism, exhausted her. When her health declined

in the early 1960s, she returned to New York to live with her daughter. She died there in 1962.

At an exhibition of African American art in 1967, the largest ever held up to that time, Savage's spirit could be detected.

| Augusta Savage

Masterworks

1923	*W. E. B. Du Bois*
1929	*Gamin*
1930	*Marcus Garvey*
1932	*Terpsichore at Rest (Reclining Nude)*
1934	*Gwendolyn Knight*
1935	*Realization*
1939	*Lift Every Voice and Sing*
1943	*The Pugilist*

Many of the artworks were by her former students. According to collage artist **Romare Bearden** (see entry), the work that "attracted the most attention, the most favorable comments, was *Gamin* ... created by Augusta Savage." Though often thwarted in her own artistic desires, her refusal to bow to the racism she encountered and her commitment to the black community, as well as the beauty of her sculpture, have remained an inspiration to artists of all colors.

Georges Seurat

Born December 2, 1859
Paris, France
Died March 29, 1891
Paris, France

George Seurat's primary contribution to the world of art was his attempt to develop a scientific approach to impressionist notions of color and light. Many of his paintings were experiments to this end. Through the course of these trials, he developed a technique known as **pointillism.** Seurat was highly respected by other artists of his time, and his work has been greatly influential in the development of modern painting. Several of his paintings, especially *A Sunday Afternoon on the Island of La Grande Jatte,* have remained extremely popular over the years.

Friends and acquaintances of Georges-Pierre Seurat found him rather difficult to penetrate. From his father, Chrysostome-Antoine Seurat, he inherited a serious and quiet temperament. Chrysostome Seurat was a minor legal official in Paris, a position which afforded his family a comfortable, middle-class life. Seurat's mother, Ernestine Faivre Seurat, was also a quiet person, but quite affectionate. She devoted her life to homemaking

"The purity of the element of the spectrum is the keystone of technique. Since I first held a brush, I had been looking for a formula of optical painting."

and raising Seurat and his much older brother and sister. Seurat was close to his mother throughout his life. He was widely regarded as exacting, well organized, intelligent, and very private.

Abandoned prestigious art school

Seurat showed considerable talent for drawing when he was young. He was encouraged by an uncle and by the time he was 15, he had decided to focus on art as a profession. He left school and enrolled in a local academy of drawing, where he studied for roughly three years. The curriculum was traditional; Seurat spent much of his class time copying statuary and drawings by famous masters of the past. Then, his talent and skill earned him admission to the best art school in France, the Ecole des Beaux Arts (School of Fine Arts). But he spent only a year there, perhaps realizing that there was not much more he could learn from the conservative orientation of the school. His real interest by then was outside school; indeed, Seurat was intrigued by the new style that had become the talk of Paris. It was called **impressionism.**

Seurat and other young artists at this time, around 1880, were fascinated by the innovations of older artists like **Claude Monet** (see entry) and Camille Pissarro. The works of these "impressionists," which were distinguished by flickering brush strokes, vivid color, and an emphasis on the play of natural light on outdoor settings, was a far cry from the classical offerings he studied at school. Seurat spent much of his student days reading about the new science of color theory. He was fascinated by the relationships among color, light, and the way the human eye perceives images. He concluded that the color effects the impressionists were trying to achieve could be controlled by fixed, almost mathematical laws. Seurat devoted his career to establishing a system of "optical painting."

After serving a year of required military service when he was 20, Seurat settled down to a methodical exploration of the theories he was developing. For two years he worked mostly in black and white. He was trying to master the exact contrasts and grades of tone in black and white before addressing color. These drawings already demonstrated a unique style. There are no obvious outlines, crosshatch markings, or even details. The figures seem little more than smudges, with areas of dark and light giving them form. Art critic and writer John Russell described Seurat's drawings as modulating "from the deepest, most velvety blacks right through to the natural white of the paper" and ventured, "no longer are we conscious of individual pencil-strokes, but merely of a process of uninterrupted *becoming*." The subjects of these drawings were ordinary ones: women sewing, farmers, simple landscapes. Seurat's friend and colleague Paul Signac, called them "the most beautiful painters' drawings there are." Seurat continued drawing throughout his life, but this early period was key to his development as a painter.

Representing form through color

The next phase of Seurat's artistic development centered on his work with oil paint and color. Around 1883 he began working on his first major painting to incorporate his theoretical formula. The large canvas, which he finished in 1884, was called *The Bathers (Une Baignade)*. Seurat produced many drawings and paintings as studies in preparation for the larger work. Each of the five main figures and the riverside landscape were carefully planned. The painting presents many elements of impressionist style, but it also reveals early evidence of Seurat's representation of form through contrasts of complimentary colors, such as red/green, blue/orange, purple/yellow, and so on.

The Bathers was rejected by the government-run **Salon** exhibition of 1884. But it was shown at an exhibit organized by a group of independent painters. This assemblage, of which Seurat was a member, rejected the power that traditional painters and critics had over who could exhibit art. Another member of the group was Signac, an artist slightly younger than Seurat. The two became friends immediately and worked together for many years. It was Signac who persuaded Seurat to use only primary colors in his paintings. Others soon began to notice Seurat's work and discuss his ideas. Not a particularly social person, however, Seurat himself spent most of his time in the studio; Signac was the one who spread the news about his colleague's experiments.

A Sunday Afternoon on the Island of La Grande Jatte, 1885. Oil on canvas, approx. 8'9" x 10'. Art Institute of Chicago, Helen Birch Bartlett Memorial Collection. Reproduced by permission of AP/Wide World Photos.

Seurat took his philosophies of light, color, and optics even further in his next and most famous painting, *A Sunday Afternoon on the Island of La Grande Jatte,* often called simply *La Grande Jatte.* As soon as he had finished *The Bathers,* Seurat began producing studies of the landscape and people on an island in the River Seine, near Paris, known as La Grande Jatte. It was a popular place to spend an afternoon strolling, fishing, and relaxing. The huge canvas took Seurat more than a year to complete. It now hangs at the Art Institute of Chicago and is one of the most popular works there. In fact, what is perhaps Seurat's most enduring image has widely permeated contemporary popular culture, spawning reproductions on everything from calendars to coffee mugs and even inspiring a prize-winning Broadway musical.

La Grande Jatte

The singular nature of *La Grande Jatte* is characterized by the rigid and methodical way in which it was painted. The canvas is covered with a surface pattern of small dots, the colors of which define the shading and outlines of the figures, trees, boats, and water. The discrete spots of color are mixed together by the viewer's eye to create a "magical atmosphere," in the words of art historian H. H. Arnason. The canvas seems to vibrate and shimmer much like the air would on a hot sunny day. Viewers and critics over the years have seized on various aspects of the painting: its spectacular illustration of contemporary color theories; its modern, geometric, abstract look; its observation of Parisian life in the 1880s. But perhaps the fundamental fascination with *La Grande Jatte* is the difficulty of comprehending that the artist could paint such a grand and beautiful painting with only tiny dots of color. Clearly, the work is more than just a collection of dots, or points. Indeed, an important critic of Seurat's time wrote that if just anyone "were to study treatises on optics for all eternity he could never paint *La Grande Jatte*." Its unique spirit and underlying creativity stem as much from Seurat's innate artistry as they do from scientific theory.

As was the case with the impressionists, Seurat's ideas and paintings were considered radical. But in the mid-1880s, he began to acquire a following of artists who believed that his style, called pointillism, divisionism, or neo-impressionism, was an important new step in the development of modern art. Signac, Pissarro, **Vincent van Gogh,** and **Paul Gauguin** (see entries) were among them. Each helped to spread Seurat's gospel. Neo-impressionist groups were formed throughout Europe, a great many in Belgium alone.

After completion of *La Grande Jatte,* Seurat painted other works that explored different aspects of pointillism. *Les Poseuses,* comprised of three women in varying poses, probed the intricacies of line and surface pattern. In *La Parade* and *Le Chahut,* Seurat's treatment of space and geometry became more abstract. His painting *The Eiffel Tower,* which depicts the Parisian monument under construction, embodies the modern use of flattened space and intense color. During this time Seurat also painted many landscapes and continued to expand the boundaries of contemporary painting through pattern and repeated imagery.

Toward the end of his life, Seurat developed suspicions about his followers; he believed they were borrowing his meth-

ods and not giving him due credit for the advances of pointillism. By the late 1880s many of them had gone on to modify Seurat's innovations, ultimately creating their own styles. Seurat died suddenly when he was only 31 years old. It is now thought that he was stricken by meningitis, an inflammation of the brain and spinal cord. Art historians have speculated widely as to what Seurat could have accomplished had he lived. Less uncertain is the immense influence his work has had on the art produced since his death. The great modern masters, among them **Pablo Picasso, Marcel Duchamp, Wassily Kandinsky** (see entries), and many others found immeasurable inspiration in Seurat's work. To be sure, his elegant amalgam of science and art was critical to the development of twentieth-century art.

Masterworks

1884	*The Bathers (Une Baignade)*
1885	*A Sunday Afternoon on the Island of La Grande Jatte*
1888	*Les Poseuses*
1889	*The Eiffel Tower*
1890	*Le Chahut*
1891	*Woman Powdering Herself*
	The Circus

◀ Le Chahut, *1890. Courtauld Institute Galleries, London. Reproduced by permission of Giraudon/Art Resource, NY.*

Alfred Stieglitz

Born in 1864
Hoboken, New Jersey
Died July 13, 1946
New York, New York

"Photography is my passion. The search for truth is my obsession."

Alfred Stieglitz's influence on the world of art and of art photography was enormous. He is credited with bringing photography into the modern era and fostering its acceptance as an art form. He was the first photographer to have his works hung in almost every major museum in the United States. Stieglitz was also an important promoter of many American and European modern artists at a time when modern art was not widely respected in the United States. He truly became a legend in his own time, revered by a cult of young artists. From 1902 until the mid-1940s, Stieglitz reigned as the central figure of American art photography.

Stieglitz's parents immigrated to the United States from Germany in 1849. Alfred was the oldest of their six children. The family enjoyed a comfortable life. The value of education and cultural awareness was highly important to the Stieglitzes, who passed these ideals on to their children. The family moved to New York City when Stieglitz was about nine years old. He attended public and private schools. When he was 17, he enrolled in the City College of New York to study engineering because a professor had told his father that it was a good profession. He went to Germany in 1881 to continue his engineering studies.

"Fools around" with first camera

According to the *New York Times,* Stieglitz saw a simple box camera in the window of a shop on a visit to Berlin. "I bought it," he recalled, "carried it to my room and began to fool around with it. It fascinated me, first as a passion, then as an obsession. The camera was waiting for me by predestination." The purchase was a turning point in Stieglitz's life; from then on his attention was absorbed by photography and the visual arts. He spent ten years in Europe, learning about photography, photographing a variety of subjects, and winning prizes in competitions.

Stieglitz's photography was unique because he was able to manipulate the camera to achieve results previously thought impossible. He took pictures at night, in snowstorms and in rain, and he was a pioneer of color photography. He also photographed just what he saw, declining to arrange scenes or alter negatives to produce a desired effect. This "straight" photography, as he called it, was revolutionary at the time. His primary goal was to capture a mood rather than an event. He was known to stand for days on a traffic island in order to snap exactly the shot he wanted. His artist's eye enabled him to capture the patterns, geometry, and beauty of urban images and in so doing, allowed him to powerfully present his vision of the modern world.

By the time Stieglitz returned to New York in 1891, his reputation had been established. Two of his most popular photographs were taken the next year: *Winter—Fifth Avenue* and *The Terminal—Street Car Horses.* The first presents a horse-drawn trolley coming up the street in a blizzard. The second depicts a streetcar driver watering his horses on a frigid morning. These subjects were considered inappropriate for artistic

The Steerage, *1907. Chloride print, 11 cm x 9.2 cm. The Art Institute of Chicago, Alfred Steiglitz Collection (1949.705). Photograph © 1994, The Art Institute of Chicago, All Rights Reserved.*

treatment in photography. They were too common, not "beautiful." With these compositions Stieglitz began to wage what he called his "battle" to make photography an artform, not simply a decoration. He used his photographs and writings to convince people that photography could be as "artistic" and expressive as other forms.

Mentors artists through 291 Gallery

Stieglitz became editor of several photography journals, the best known called *Camera Work*. He also organized and judged national exhibitions of photography and opened a gallery at 291 Fifth Avenue in New York for exhibitions of the work of his colleagues in a group called the Photo-Secessionists. (A secessionist is one who formally withdraws from an organization.) The 291 Gallery became the central show and meeting place for a generation of photographers. Stieglitz eventually exhibited the work of painters and sculptors there as well. He discovered and furthered the careers of American artists Paul Strand, John Marin, Arthur Dove, and Marsden Hartley, as well as photographer **Ansel Adams** and painter **Georgia O'Keeffe** (see entries), whom he married in 1924. Many young artists were drawn to the forceful personality and energy of Stieglitz, who believed passionately in the progressive direction of modern art. Stieglitz was the first to introduce to America the works of important European modern artists like **Pablo Picasso** and **Henri Matisse** (see entries).

After World War I and into the 1920s, Stieglitz occupied himself with a variety of projects. He spent more than 20 years creating portraits of Georgia O'Keeffe; he took thousands of photos of her performing household tasks, painting, and sewing. He also undertook photographic studies of her neck, feet, torso, and hands. One writer attested of this series, "No more comprehensive or intimate photographic essay has ever been made of one human being." During these years Stieglitz also began collecting photographs. He bought as many early and contemporary prints as he could and accepted gifts from his many photographer friends. He eventually donated his collection to the Metropolitan Museum in

New York, which formed the bedrock of what would become a world-class assemblage.

In the early 1920s Stieglitz began what he called his "Equivalents" series, in which he photographed images of the sky and clouds to demonstrate that in art, one can express emotion and meaning through form as well as subject. Just as children find shapes of animals in clouds, Stieglitz used his camera to find light and patterns in the sky that reflected the equivalent of his feelings. Another such series was comprised of views of New York skyscrapers, all taken from the window of the hotel in which Stieglitz lived at the time. These photos are notable for the abstract designs of light and shadow reflected on the buildings.

Would not accept payment for photographs

In the late 1920s Stieglitz opened another gallery in New York, called An American Place. Here he exhibited his own photographs as well as the photos, paintings, and sculptures of numerous other artists. The gallery remained open until his death in 1946, though poor health prevented him from working in 1937. When lack of funds threatened to close the gallery, a public appeal raised enough money to keep it afloat. Stieglitz did not accept payment for his own photographs. But he made many other artists famous and some even wealthy by displaying their works in his gallery.

In 1934 a group of more than 20 writers and artists collaborated to publish a book of their impressions of Stieglitz. Titled *America and Alfred Stieglitz,* the volume contains tributes to the photographer in his roles as artist, philosopher, and art world prophet. The authors describe his quaint dress: a drab gray suit and flowing black cape, a wispy tie and pancake hat. They remember his gift of gab, several even referring to him as a "showman." They also describe his deep love of art and tremendous generosity. It was widely reported that Stieglitz would not sell a work of art unless he was certain the piece would be "happy" with the buyer.

In his later years Stieglitz was called "the father of modern photography, the greatest photographer in the world, and the founder of modern art in America." He received many honors, including the progress medal from the Royal Photographic Society in London and a citation from the City College of New York. Indeed, Stieglitz's place in twentieth-century art was remarkable. In his dual role as artist and mentor, ventured one writer, "He probably has had a more profound influence on the course of [art] photography in America than any other single individual."

Masterworks

1893	*Winter—Fifth Avenue*
	The Terminal—Street Car Horses
1903	*The Flat Iron Building*
1904	*The New York Central Docks*
1907	*The Steerage*
1931	*From the Shelton Westward—New York*

Henry O. Tanner

Born June 21, 1859
Pittsburgh, Pennsylvania
Died May 25, 1937
Paris, France

"Religious themes were for Tanner, like Rembrandt, very personal modes of expression."

James K. Kettlewell

▲ *Portrait: Reproduced by permission of NYT Pictures.*

Henry O. Tanner longed to be an artist from the age of 12. While walking with his father one day in Philadelphia's Fairmount Park, he stopped to watch a landscape painter at work. Inspired, he returned home and fashioned his first canvas out of an old awning, punching a whole in the cover of a discarded geography book for his first palette. So began the long career of the foremost African American painter of the turn of the twentieth century.

Tanner was born on June 21, 1859, in Pittsburgh, Pennsylvania, but was raised in Philadelphia. He was the first of seven children born to Sarah Miller Tanner and Benjamin Tucker Tanner, a minister and, later, bishop in the African Methodist Episcopal Church. Sarah Tanner was born into slavery (the granddaughter of a white plantation owner) but escaped north by way of the Underground Railroad network of slave smugglers and was raised in freedom. Benjamin Tanner was born to a family that had been free for several generations. He was able to attend college and a theological seminary. The younger Tanner grew up with the many advantages of education that few African Americans of his time enjoyed. His middle name, Ossawa, was given in honor of Osawatomie, Kansas, the town where abolitionist John Brown killed five slavery sympathizers three years before Tanner's birth.

Hampered by racial discrimination

Tanner taught himself to paint. His favorite subjects were seascapes and harbor views, as well as town scenes and animals. In 1876, when he visited the Centennial Exposition in Philadelphia and saw the work of other African American artists such as Edmonia Lewis and Edward Bannister, he became certain of his chosen career. Four years later Tanner was accepted at the Philadelphia Academy of Fine Arts, where he became a student of the highly regarded **realist** painter Thomas Eakins. Tanner's work progressed under Eakins, who taught him how to render the human form, use light and shadow to express mood, and probe the depths of his subject. But like so many black artists of his generation and those to follow, Tanner suffered from racial discrimination. He exhibited paintings in several shows, but he was seldom able to sell any.

It was extremely difficult for African American artists to achieve success in the late nineteenth century; they labored outside the mainstream art world, and few blacks were wealthy enough to become patrons of the arts. There were thus few institutions to help black artists. Moreover, the themes, events, and expressions of African American life that an artist like Tanner strove to illuminate did not appeal to many white viewers.

After two years at art school, Tanner decided to travel and study in Europe. He made several attempts to raise money for the trip, among them selling paintings and photographs in Philadelphia and opening a photo studio in Atlanta, Georgia. But none of his schemes worked. He was finally able to embark for the Continent when Bishop Joseph Hartzell of Cincinnati arranged an exhibition of his works and then purchased all of the paintings as a show of support. Tanner sailed for Europe on January

4, 1891. He intended to go to Rome, where Edmonia Lewis had found success, but he stopped in Paris first and was soon swept up by the excitement of the art world there. Finding none of the racial tension he had experienced in the United States, he stayed for two years, painting landscapes in the countryside and focusing on traditional African American themes, particularly "lesson" paintings, a genre that features the handing down of a skill or knowledge by an older person to the next generation.

Reinvented depiction of blacks with *Banjo Lesson*

In 1892 Tanner became ill and returned to Philadelphia. During his long recuperation period, he contemplated religion, prejudice in the United States, and the place of African Americans in the art world. It was during this time that he painted his most famous work, *The Banjo Lesson,* which shows an elderly man teaching a boy to play the banjo. The painting set an example of depicting African Americans in a serious, dignified manner, unlike the cartoonish way they were often portrayed—particularly by white artists—in much American art of the period.

Tanner was urged by such African American leaders as Booker T. Washington to stay in the United States and devote himself and his art to political and social causes. But he was certain that Paris was the best place for him to develop as an artist and make his mark. *The Banjo Lesson* was among the last of his African American-oriented work; after returning eagerly to Paris in 1894, Tanner began painting biblical themes and continued in this endeavor for the rest of his life.

Tanner saw great achievement and activity throughout the 1890s. Several of his paintings were accepted at the prestigious yearly Paris **Salon** exhibitions, and one was awarded a medal in 1897. This painting, *The Raising of Lazarus,* was purchased by the French government; only two other American artists, John Singer Sargent and James McNeill Whistler, had ever been so honored. In 1899 Tanner married Jessie Macauley Olssen, a Swedish musician who had been raised in San Francisco. They had a

son, Jesse Ossawa Tanner, who was born in 1903. Except for two years spent in New York, the Tanners would remain in Paris.

By the early 1900s Tanner's paintings were so popular in both France and the United States that the artist found it difficult to keep up with the demand. In 1902 the popular magazine *Ladies' Home Journal* used his paintings for the covers of four issues. Six years later, 35 of his paintings were exhibited in New York.

Influenced by Middle Eastern culture and World War I

Tanner's travels throughout the Middle East in 1897 and 1898 and to North Africa in 1908 and the years prior to World

Abraham's Oak, 1905. Oil on canvas, 21⅝" x 28⅝". National Museum of American Art, Smithsonian Institution. Gift of Mr. and Mrs. Norman Robbins. Reproduced by permission of National Museum of American Art, Washington, DC/Art Resource, NY.

Masterworks

1893	*The Banjo Lesson*
1894	*The Thankful Poor*
1895	*The Young Sabot Maker*
1896	*Daniel in the Lion's Den*
1897	*The Raising of Lazarus*
1898	*The Annunciation*
1899	*Flight into Egypt*
1906	*Disciples at Emmaus*
1918	*American Red Cross Canteen, Toul, France, WWI*
1932	*The Burning of Sodom and Gomorrah*

War I deeply influenced the content and style of his work. He was attracted to the exotic Islamic art found there and to the colorful street scenes of the cities. He would recall the native textiles, ceramics, and white-washed, stone-floored buildings in later interior scenes.

But the outbreak of war in 1914 interrupted Tanner's work. He served with the American Red Cross in France from 1917, when the United States entered the war, until 1919. Deeply moved by the horrors he experienced, he painted a number of large pieces about the war and presented three to the Red Cross, including *American Red Cross Canteen, Toul, France, WWI*.

After the war Tanner returned to biblical scenes, and his reputation continued to grow. He received numerous honors and awards, including the Chevalier of the Legion of Honor, the highest award presented by the French government. His work was shown in New York, Boston, and Chicago, and his paintings were purchased by several museums for their permanent collections. In the early 1920s a group of African American artists established the Tanner Art League to sponsor exhibitions of African American art, and many younger artists went to visit or study with the respected master in Paris.

Still, despite his popularity, Tanner's work was not without criticism. A few African Americans, particularly those prominent during the Harlem Renaissance of the 1920s, felt that Tanner should have concentrated more on African American themes. And by the 1930s his works were considered old-fashioned by the young artists who embraced the new styles of cubism and surrealism. After Tanner's death in 1937, his work was almost forgotten.

But in the late 1960s interest in Tanner was revived; the first major exhibition of his work in the United States took place in 1969. Cosponsored by the Frederick Douglas Institute and the National Collection of Fine Arts, the exhibit featured 90 oils, watercolors, drawings, and **etchings.** After opening in Washington, D.C., it traveled to seven American museums, thus becoming the first one-man show by an African American artist to tour the country's major museums. In 1991, nearly a century after he painted his *Banjo Lesson,* a major retrospective of Tanner's work was sponsored by the Philadelphia Museum of Art, refocusing attention on this great African American artist who was forced by racism to spend most of his adult life in France.

Titian

Born 1488 (some sources say 1490)
Pieve di Cadore, Italy
Died August 27, 1576
Venice, Italy

"He was principally and first of all a painter, but a painter whose handling of paint equalled Michelangelo's mastery of draughtsmanship."

E. H. Gombrich

During his half-century career, the work of Italian painter Titian dominated that discipline in Venice. Among his diverse talents were portraiture, the depiction of landscapes, and the representation of scenes from the Bible and classical mythology. His singular, innovative style was admired for its use of brilliant color, powerful movement, and dramatic feeling. He also introduced new techniques of oil painting, which brought added richness and freedom to the medium. Titian's influence on later artists, including nineteenth-century French painter Eugene Delacroix, Dutch master **Rembrandt van Rijn,** Flemish painter **Peter Paul Rubens,** and French painter **Edouard Manet** (see entries), has continued to exert its force for four centuries.

Tiziano Vecelli, who became known simply as Titian, was born in a small town in the foothills of the Alps north of Venice. His father, Gregorio Vecelli, took the budding artist to Venice when he was about ten years old to become an apprentice in the workshop of a mosaic artist. But it was clear very early that the boy's interests and talent lay in painting. Eventually he began working in the studios of well-known painters, such as Gentile Bellini and, later, Giovanni Bellini. His most important teacher, however, was the much-admired Giorgone, who taught Titian about the principles of color and light and also introduced him to the new school of landscape painting. They worked together on **frescoes** for an important building in Venice in 1508. Giorgone died shortly thereafter, still a young man.

Appointed state painter

Titian's skill with a brush soon became widely known and after the death of Giovanni Bellini in 1516, he was appointed state painter by the government of Venice. His fame was cemented two years later when he painted the *Assumption of the Virgin* for the city's Church of Santa Maria dei Frari. This work astounded viewers with its vivid color, especially the red of the Virgin's robes and the intensely focused golden light coming from above. Rather than portraying a traditionally static scene, with little movement or emotion, Titian presented three levels of swirling figures and draperies, outstretched arms and glowing faces, all depicted as if the viewer were looking up at the scene from below. Taken together, these components suggested a religious awe unprecedented in painting.

The technical abilities and florid style of this unorthodox artist confounded his contemporaries. Painting in oils was not very common then; Titian's impressive use of the medium brought it into favor. He would go over each canvas several times, accumulating details and building elements with color. Over the years his brush strokes became freer and looser, quite unlike the controlled, tightly spaced strokes of the traditional style. Furthermore, he employed the texture of the paint itself to create a lush effect. He was even known to use his fingers instead of a brush. Titian treated each painting with a layer of varnish, which he mixed himself, to give it a glossy finish.

The Pesaro Madonna,
1526. Approx. 16' x 9'.
Santa Maria dei Frari,
Venice.

Soon the name of the exciting Venetian painter was on everyone's lips. He was consistently noted as the instigator of a revolutionary change in painting style and technique. He received commissions from many churches and from wealthy patrons who wanted their portraits painted or contracted for a "votive" scene that portrayed themselves and their families with an important religious figure, such as the Virgin Mary or a patron saint. Titian's patrons were among the most powerful families of the various city-states of Italy, including the Urbino, Ferrara, and Mantua clans. His fame quickly spread to the royal courts of Italy and western Europe.

Titian was a savvy businessman as well as a gifted artist. He frequently arranged with patrons to exchange artworks for a trading license or a pension for one of his sons. Nonetheless, some of the nobles did not fulfill their parts of these agreements, and Titian occasionally found himself in financial trouble. Many letters survive respectfully imploring this duke or that cardinal to send him promised funds.

Becomes favorite of Emperor Charles V

In the early 1530s Emperor Charles V, King of Spain and ruler of a large part of western Europe, visited northern Italy. He had heard of Titian's work and commissioned a portrait. When it was finished he was so pleased that he made Titian a nobleman and gave him the title of Knight of the Golden Spur. It was said that from then on Charles would let no other artist paint his portrait; he regularly summoned Titian to his court to capture his likeness. Charles V was also a patron of **Albrecht Dürer** (see entry), the great German engraver and wood-block specialist, and it is possible that Titian met Dürer when the German visited Venice in 1505.

Charles's son and successor to the throne, Philip II, was also a great admirer of Titian and collected many of his paintings. A large part of his collection was housed in the Escorial, the Spanish royal palace, where it was viewed and studied by later painters, among them court painter **Diego Velazquez** and the Flemish master **Peter Paul Rubens** (see entries). At Philip's

request, Titian undertook a series of paintings called "poesies" in which he depicted scenes from ancient mythology. Two of these were *Venus and Adonis* and *The Rape of Europa.* He had done paintings of such non-religious subjects for other patrons earlier in his career. These depictions are noteworthy for their unusual use of **perspective** and beautiful landscapes. Perhaps even more significant, however, are the marked sensuality and emotion displayed in the figures portrayed; viewers feel as if they could almost reach out and touch a living being caught in the canvas. The posture of one famous reclining nude, the *Venus of Urbino,* was copied by Manet three hundred years later for his scandalous painting *Olympia.*

Along with his religious and mythological paintings, Titian was celebrated for his portraits. He painted many of the most powerful figures of his time, his unique skill and probing intellect enabling him to reveal the sitter's character as well as physical features. Viewers can sense the romantic nature and sadness of the *Man with the Glove.* Similarly, in his *Portrait of Pope Paul III with His Grandsons,* Titian depicts the frail, elderly pontiff, whose eyes nonetheless retain a wily intelligence, thus suggesting something of the subject's political capabilities. The faces of the two young men, too, seem to hint at a complicated relationship to their grandfather in the context of his vaunted position.

Visited Rome in his sixties

Titian painted the Pope Paul III scene during his only trip to Rome, in about 1545. He was in his sixties when he first saw the work of the **Renaissance** master **Michelangelo** (see entry). It is possible that he may have actually met Michelangelo during this visit; more certain is that Titian admired his painting and sculpture and may have been influenced by them to some degree. In the years following this journey, Titian perfected what was called the grand portrait style, which was copied by Rubens,

◀ Portrait of Pope Paul III with His Grandsons, *1545. Gallerie Nazionali di Capodimonte, Naples. Reproduced by permission of Alinari/Art Resource, NY.*

his student Sir Anthony Van Dyck, and the majority of portrait artists for years to come.

Toward the end of his life, Titian painted many religious paintings of a deeply personal and almost mystical nature. He used very loose brush strokes, lending his figures a spiritual quality, particularly in comparison to the dense, muscular flesh displayed on the frames of subjects in his earlier works. The source of light in paintings like his *Pietà* are ambiguous and add a theatricality to the scene. In this painting, Titian's last, he included a portrait of himself as St. Jerome. Toward the end of his life Titian headed a large workshop manned by many assistants, some of whom became great painters in their own right, including Tintoretto, Veronese, and **El Greco** (see entry).

Titian's freedom with both his materials and style was truly unusual in his day. One writer of the era described his body of work as aggregates of paint splotches and scratches when viewed up close but which, at a distance, become a "magical" combination of form and color. The artist's penchant for patchy light and color prefigured the more abstract renderings of the impressionists—who lived and worked roughly three centuries later. Like these spiritual children would, Titian harnessed his gifts to express his feelings about the natural world and religion in a way no painter had before. His impact in his own time—and ours—is incalculable.

Henri de Toulouse-Lautrec

Born November 24, 1864
Albi, France
Died September 9, 1901
Malromé, France

O f all the artists who made their mark in turn-of-the-century France, Henri de Toulouse-Lautrec's view of 1890s Paris is perhaps the most sensitive and compellingly human. During the height of his career he produced hundreds of paintings, drawings, and posters celebrating the entertainers and other characters whom he met at nightclubs, bordellos, and theaters. That he was physically disabled allowed him acceptance into areas of this world where an able-bodied person might have been an intruder. His keen sense of observation and empathy for all kinds of people are just two of the elements that make Toulouse-Lautrec's work unique. Like other painters following in the wake of the impressionists, he forged his own modern style, one that remains recognized and admired today.

Henri-Marie-Raymond de Toulouse-Lautrec-Monfa came from an aristocratic and wealthy family in the south of France. His father, Comte Alphonse de Toulouse-Lautrec, was a sports-

"In spite of his personal tragedy, Toulouse-Lautrec paints with sanity, vigor, and the clearest, sharpest perception of the life around him."

John Canaday

man and artist known for eccentric behavior. Toulouse-Lautrec's mother was a quiet, cultured woman. She provided the boy with his early education and cared for him throughout his life. Theirs was a tightly knit extended family; one of Toulouse-Lautrec's cousins would be his lifelong friend.

Bone disease and fractures stunted growth

Toulouse-Lautrec was plagued by poor health early on. He developed a bone disease when he was a child that slowed his growth. Then, when he was 13, he fractured his left leg; a year later he fractured the right. Neither of the breaks healed properly, and the young man's legs ceased to grow from that point. Because his upper body developed normally, his child-size legs were forced to support and balance an adult torso. For the rest of his life Toulouse-Lautrec had trouble walking, though he was a very strong swimmer. He was regarded as a lively, affectionate, and kind person. Despite his disability, Toulouse-Lautrec pursued his dream of a career in art and became quite successful. With his family's money behind him, he could focus on his work without the distraction of having to earn a living. This undoubtedly afforded him the freedom to experiment.

Sporting pastimes, like horseback riding, horse racing, and hunting, were very important to the Toulouse-Lautrec family. Sketching and drawing was an acceptable hobby, and young Toulouse-Lautrec enjoyed drawing pictures of horses and jockeys. When his leg fractures and other health problems kept him in bed for long periods as a teenager, he began to view his efforts with more seriousness. He took painting and drawing lessons with a local sporting artist. When he was 17 Toulouse-Lautrec went to study in Paris, where his training followed the traditional path.

But in Paris Toulouse-Lautrec was also exposed to the controversial new style that was developing: it was called **impressionism.** Painters like **Claude Monet, Pierre-Auguste Renoir** (see entries), and Camille Pissarro were beginning to attract attention by holding their own exhibitions. Toulouse-Lautrec was similarly intrigued by **Edouard Manet**'s (see entry) open-air paintings and the work of Edgar Degas, especially his depictions of dancers, horse races, and city life. Toulouse-Lautrec moved on to a different instruction studio in 1883. There he met other young painters, including the Dutch artist **Vincent van Gogh** (see entry). Toulouse-Lautrec and van Gogh became friends and worked together occasionally. They were influenced by many of the same ideas about art, and both had tempestuous inner lives that they longed to commit to canvas. The two painters nonetheless developed very different styles.

The 1880s saw Toulouse-Lautrec auditioning a variety of styles. Many of his early paintings, including a portrait of his mother reading, are reminiscent of the impressionist paintings of the day. Another key influence of this time was Japanese art. Toulouse-Lautrec adopted many of the elements of Japanese prints, among them decorative patterns, broad areas of color, tilted viewpoints, and a reliance on outline and silhouette. His first work to incorporate these concepts was *Cirque Fernando: The Equestrienne*. It demonstrates a major shift from impressionism, as well as the suggestion of paintings by **Georges Seurat** and **Paul Gauguin** (see entries).

Developed spontaneous, colorful style

By 1888, however, Toulouse-Lautrec had developed his own techniques and signature style, which changed little over the remaining dozen years of his life. He employed a free style of brush stroke and favored long sweeping outlines. His colors were usually bold and brilliant—greens, oranges, and highlights of red. Sometimes he used color for emphasis, applying it with little regard to how it actually appeared in the scene he portrayed. This was an important innovation that influenced later artists. On the whole, Toulouse-Lautrec's style was highly spontaneous and brimming with vitality, a perfect mode for illustrating the "slices of life" he observed in the nightlife of Paris.

Toulouse-Lautrec's work was also characterized by his production of posters and **lithographs.** Poster art was becoming very popular in the 1890s. Toulouse-Lautrec created posters to advertise entertainers at the cafés and art exhibitions. He was

probably the first "serious" painter to work in advertising. Posters and other drawings were often printed by a method called lithography, in which drawings are made on a specially prepared stone with a brush or pen. The stone is treated with acid in the areas where there is no drawing. Then a greasy ink is rolled onto the stone; the ink does not stick to the acid-treated surfaces. Pressure is then applied to print the inked sections onto paper. Toulouse-Lautrec developed several lithography techniques. In fact, alterations to his style were inspired by the requirements for making a good print. His efforts were influential on commercial, or printed, art for many years.

Toulouse-Lautrec's work of the 1890s represents the apex of his career. He produced hundreds of pieces, working hard during the day and frequenting the cafés for observation and cocktails each night. He also attended the theater and circuses. Moreover, he observed court trials and surgery in the operating theaters of a doctor friend. He sketched people and scenes wherever he went. Occasionally Toulouse-Lautrec visited bordellos, where the prostitutes of the era plied their trade. He befriended and observed the women who lived and worked there. *The Salon in the Rue des Moulins,* a view of a bordello, is considered one of his masterpieces. Toulouse-Lautrec depicts the women's lives frankly and straightforwardly, with beautiful colors and inviting composition.

Observer—and mainstay—of Paris nightlife

The preciseness of his work makes clear that Toulouse-Lautrec was no mere observer of this world of theaters and nightclubs—he lived it as well. As he grew older, he spent more and more time at bars and dance halls. His drinking, in fact, began to negatively affect his health, which was never good. His mental health suffered as well. In early 1899 Toulouse-Lautrec had a breakdown. He spent a few months in a hospital, and his recovery was fairly quick. He used drawings he did from memory of circus scenes to convince doctors that his mental health had improved. At the end of 1899 he began to work seriously again, but he also resumed his romance with the bottle. His work from this period is darker and seems more labored. In the spring of 1901 Toulouse-Lautrec suffered another breakdown; he died in September of that year at the age of 37.

The "life" that Toulouse-Lautrec left behind in his art is an exciting, colorful, busy one, but one often tinged with sadness and loneliness. The man and woman depicted in *A la Mie* appear tired, most likely drunk, and seem to have nowhere to go. In his paintings and light, sketchy drawings Toulouse-Lautrec presents actors, dancers, and music hall singers performing, socializing, or resting backstage. Many of them appear weary, as if their best days are behind them. Toulouse-Lautrec painted and drew numerous scenes from the Moulin Rouge, one of the most popular

La Goulue Entering the Moulin Rouge, *1892. Lithograph. Reproduced by permission of Giraudon/ Art Resource, NY.*

music halls in Paris. He rendered portraits of the young actress May Belfort, popular singer Yvette Guilbert, and dancer Jean Avril. He depicted the patrons of the nightlife establishments, many of whom were his friends and acquaintances. In all of these we see individuals, with cares and emotions on their faces, all looking to entertain or have a good time. Toulouse-Lautrec tried to reveal human lives and human activities in a sympathetic manner; in viewing each of his works, one can detect the mystery, romance, or despair of the subject.

The reach of Toulouse-Lautrec's paintings and lithographs was great. His colors and designs inspired the style of **fauvism** and exerted themselves on artists like Maurice Vlaminck and **Henri Matisse.** His work was also an important influence on the career of **Pablo Picasso** (see entries), especially his early work in Paris. Indeed, Toulouse-Lautrec's outpourings served as a link between many of the experiments of late nineteenth-century art and the early expressionist works of the twentieth century. His graphic works were important for their artistic and technical advances. All of these uniquely capture the gaiety—and pathos—that was Paris in the 1890s; many are on display at the Toulouse-Lautrec museum in the artist's hometown of Albi, France.

Masterworks

1887	*Portrait of the Comtesse A. de Toulouse-Lautrec in the Salon*
1888	*Cirque Fernando: The Equestrienne*
1889	*At the Moulin de la Galette*
1891	*A la Mie*
1892	*La Goulue Entering the Moulin Rouge*
1893-95	*At the Moulin Rouge*
1894	*The Salon in the Rue des Moulins*
1895	*Cha-U-Kao, The Female Clown*

J.M.W. Turner

Born April 23, 1775
London, England
Died December 19, 1851
London, England

"Turner makes you see and think of a great deal more than the object before you; he knows how to soothe or to intoxicate, to fire or depress, by a few notes, or forms, or colours."

William Makepeace Thackeray

J. M. W. Turner was a "modern" painter at least 50, if not 100, years ahead of his time. His emotionally charged landscapes and seascapes are more appreciated today than they were in his era. Contemporary viewers, in fact, can see glimpses of many modern styles in Turner's paintings of the 1830s and 1840s, ranging from impressionism to abstract expressionism. Another sign of his forward thinking was Turner's interest in using light and color to express the feelings inspired by nature. Such portrayals were not accepted in Turner's time and led critics to deem his paintings full of "soapsuds and whitewash." They were criticized as vulgar and unfinished. But Turner was committed to his muse, and his dogged pursuit of his vision ultimately earned him a place in art history as one of England's finest.

Joseph Mallord William Turner was known as "Billy" to his family. He was born in London and lived there all of his life, which spanned some of the most exciting events in English history—from the loss of the American Colonies through wars with Napoleon, the Industrial Revolution, and the early years of Queen Victoria's reign. London was a teeming and dirty but also lively city during Turner's childhood, and he grew up a streetwise young man. His father, also named William, was a barber and wigmaker. The family lived above his shop in a slum area marked by narrow streets. Turner spent many hours in his father's shop and on the streets, sometimes to escape the rages of his mother, Mary, who was emotionally unstable. Her outbursts created an uncomfortable atmosphere at home. Turner was very close to his father, and the two men lived together until the elder Turner's death when he was over 80 years old. He served as his son's companion and studio assistant.

Streetwise London boy bewitched by country landscape

When Turner's younger sister, Mary Ann, died at the age of eight, Mary Turner's mental state deteriorated further. It was at this time, when Turner was 11, that he was sent to live with an uncle in Brentford, a country town. There he attended school for the first time and was afforded the chance to enjoy country life—fishing, hiking, and breathing clean air. Turner developed a love of nature and landscape that remained with him throughout his life. He spent many summers from the time he was 17 until he was almost 70 taking walking and sketching trips to the countrysides of England, Wales, France, and Italy. When he returned to his parents in London at the age of 12, his father hung some drawings he had done in Brentford in his barbershop. A patron saw them and arranged for Turner to enter the school of the Royal Academy of Art.

Just a year after entering the Royal Academy school, Turner showed one of his watercolors in the Academy's annual exhibition. This was the most important art show in London. Turner placed works there almost every year for over 50 years. At art school, Turner was educated in the conservative style of eighteenth-century painting. He produced copies of ancient statuary and life-studies of nudes in a very idealized and exacting style.

◀ Portrait (p. 444): Reproduced by permission of Archive Photos.

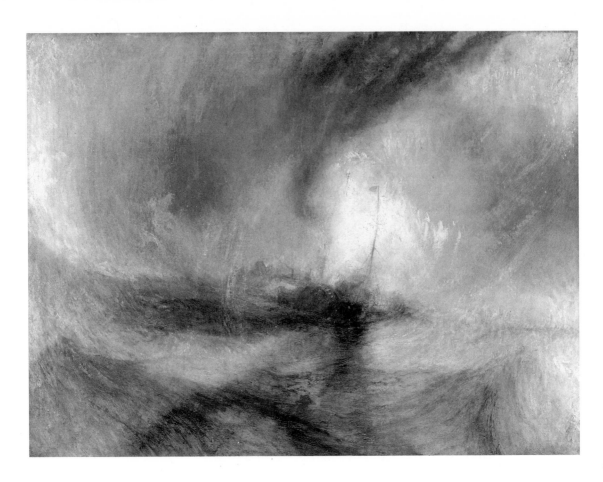

Snowstorm: Steamer off a Harbour's Mouth, *1842. Oil on canvas, 91.4 cm x 121.9 cm. Clore Collection, Tate Gallery, London/Art Resource, NY.*

Turner also took drawing classes with a local architect and earned some money coloring the prints of an engraver whose shop was near Turner's home. There he began to master watercolors, a medium which would earn him great fame.

Turner began earning money for his own **engravings** before he finished school. Drawings of landscapes were very popular; people loved picturesque views of castles, churches, farmhouses, bridges, and mountains. These scenes were printed in magazines and sold in small collections. Drawings had become widely available because they were printed as engravings, designs etched into metal, usually copper, which can then be inked and printed. Much of Turner's fortune was made from engravings. He produced over 900, from which thousands of copies were made and sold. Many of Turner's etchings stemmed from sketches of his summer travels.

While his engravings earned him a comfortable living, it was his watercolors and oil paintings that brought Turner fame. He was very active at the Royal Academy of Art after he graduated from art school; the early paintings he showed in the Academy exhibitions were watercolors of various country scenes. They were traditionally rendered and lauded by critics and Academy members. But in the mid-1790s Turner's work began to display a more personal and unique style. Along with the expected hazy blues and grays, he began to add bright yellows and reds. Greater contrasts of light and shade appeared. Though critical response remained positive, some seemed uncomfortable with the imaginative style and emotion permeating these pictures. This ambivalence would set the tone for later criticism of Turner's work. There were, however, some unequivocally harsh words throughout his career.

Lashed to mast to experience storm at sea

As a boy Turner had spent many hours along London's Thames River watching ships and boats going by. He developed a love for everything related to the sea. This was reinforced during his summer excursions. From the late 1790s on, many of his paintings focused on the sea. He painted seascapes of approaching storms, such as *Calais Pier*, and of clearing storms, such as *Light and Color: The Morning after the Deluge*. One of Turner's most celebrated works, *Snowstorm: Steamer off a Harbour's Mouth*, depicts a terrible snowstorm at sea. According to popular lore, Turner was actually aboard the steamer in question when the storm blew in; he took the opportunity to have the crew lash him to the mast so that he could experience the fury of the tempest on deck. In the painting, the viewer can hardly make out the vessel, but the swirling movement of color and dense texture of the atmosphere lend a strong impression of what the artist must have felt.

Turner, like many other artists and writers of the eighteenth century, was greatly influenced by romanticism. Explorers, scientists, and philosophers were introducing new wonders and ideas to the culture. Knowledge of the world and its people seemed limitless. Artists generally were able to travel; some

Burning of the Houses of Lords and Commons, 16th October, 1834, *1835. Clore Collection, Tate Gallery, London/Art Resource, NY.*

pursued questions of science. Most labored to capture this expansiveness in their work. Landscape painters in particular tried to render their subjects with scientific accuracy. Artists thought of their time as a new Golden Age and felt a kinship to the artists and scholars of ancient Greece and Rome. Scenes from mythology, history, and the Bible became very popular. The goal of many artists was to "see the world through the eyes of a poet."

Turner was part of this movement, yet he was able to venture beyond it. Indeed, he painted scenes from mythology, and many of his landscapes have a mysterious, passionate quality to them. But what distinguished Turner from the other romantics was his keen desire to approximate light and atmosphere, as well as his dedication to emotional expression through color. This focus connects Turner with the French **impressionism** of the nineteenth century. He even went so far as to paint out-of-doors, which the impressionist painters are often credited with spearheading—Turner beat them by 50 years. With the sweep of his brush strokes and a wealth of luminous pinks, blues, and yellows, Turner was able to capture the feeling one gets when watching water crash in a storm or the sun cut through a mist at sunrise.

Pushed boundaries with modern sensibilities

Turner became the most respected painter in England during the first half of the nineteenth century. His reputation was established with his early traditional paintings, many portraying critical events of the era such as the *Battle of Trafalgar.* And through his activities in the artistic community, he gained the further admiration of his peers. But by the 1820s Turner's image began to change; to some he was turning into a strange, eccentric man, who wore nothing but old clothes and zealously guarded his painting techniques. Critics began to lambast his paintings as unfinished. Indeed, his blobs and dabs of thick paint shocked viewers who were used to smooth, even brush strokes. His colors were denounced as too vivid and showy. A cartoon of the time shows Turner swabbing paint on a canvas with a mop. Of course, these are the same criticisms that have been aimed at modern painters throughout the twentieth century; in this, Turner's critics were also ahead of their time.

One of Turner's later works demonstrates how completely he could adapt to a changing world and yet remain true to his vision. In *Rain, Steam, and Speed,* he depicted a large steam engine crossing a bridge in a downpour of rain and thick fog. The engine seems about to hurtle off the canvas, the rain and steam smothering the composition. Turner had been painting rain for a long time, but trains were new and particularly modern—they did not exist during the artist's youth. To be sure, the world had changed enormously over the 50 years of his career. Turner seemed to admire the power of industry and invention just as he admired that of the sea and nature.

When Turner died in 1851, he was 76 years old, quite aged for his time. He had gathered a large fortune and managed to keep many of his works, which had become quite valuable. His will bestowed his life's work on the National Gallery of Britain—300 oil paintings, 300 watercolors, and roughly

Masterworks

1803	*Calais Pier, with French Poissards Preparing for Sea*
1806	*The Battle of Trafalgar as Seen from the Mizen Starboard*
1812	*Snowstorm: Hannibal and His Army Crossing the Alps*
1835	*Burning of the Houses of Lords and Commons, 16th October, 1834*
1838	*The Fighting "Temeraire" Tugged to Her Last Berth*
1840	*The Slave Ship (Slavers Throwing Overboard the Dead and Dying)*
1842	*Snowstorm: Steamer off a Harbour's Mouth*
1843	*Light and Color: The Morning after the Deluge*
1844	*Rain, Steam, and Speed: The Great Western Railway*

19,000 drawings. Turner stipulated that his works not be broken up, his will requiring the museum to add space adequate to display them. This request was not fulfilled until 1987, more than 125 years after Turner's death, when a special gallery was opened as part of the Tate Gallery in London. Despite the lateness of this grand exhibition, several generations of artists have admired Turner's work for its boundless imagination, expressiveness, and modern sensibility.

Diego Velazquez

Born in 1599
Seville, Spain
Died August 6, 1660
Madrid, Spain

The painter Velazquez enjoyed a uniquely high profile; as the official court painter for the King of Spain, he combined the careers of artist and diplomat. More than three hundred years after his death, his renderings of the Spanish royal family and the ordinary folk of Seville offer us a uniquely comprehensive view of seventeenth-century Spain. Every subsequent generation of artists has studied and admired the work of Velazquez.

Diego Rodriguez de Silva y Velazquez was the son of Juan Rodriguez de Silva and Geronima Velazquez, respected and affluent citizens of Seville. A quiet and observant child, he demonstrated a talent for drawing at an early age, often sketching scenes from the marketplace in his schoolbooks. When he was 11 years old, Velazquez was apprenticed to a well-known painter in the city, Francisco Pacheco. He lived with Pacheco and served as his assistant while acquiring formal painting techniques. Pacheco was at the center of a large group of artists, writers, and scholars who

"I would rather be an ordinary painter working from life than be the greatest copyist on earth."

▲ *Portrait:* Self-portrait. *Reproduced by permission of The Bettmann Archive.*

met often at his home for discussion and entertainment. A significant portion of the young Velazquez's education came from meeting these people and listening to their conversations.

Records common folk in tavern scenes

Pacheco was impressed by Velazquez's growing talent but disappointed by his student's lack of interest in painting the traditional religious scenes that were commissioned, or ordered, by the many churches in Seville. Instead, Velazquez longed to paint the people of Seville, market scenes, and taverns. Most of his early works are *bodegones,* from the Spanish word for tavern, meaning scenes of people engaged in everyday activities; he depicted Sevillians drinking in bars or cooking in their kitchens. Among Velazquez's most famous works of this time are *Old Woman Cooking Eggs* and *The Water Seller,* both of which he completed when he was about 19. They evidence a mastery of composition, rich color, and dramatic light in the style of sixteenth-century Italian painter Caravaggio. Velazquez invested every subject with vigor and drama, refuting the idea that town life was too mundane for preservation on canvas.

Also when he was 19, Velazquez married Juana Pacheco, his teacher's daughter, established a workshop, and took on apprentices of his own. Usually only much older artists were outfitted in this way, but Velazquez had already earned recognition as an unusual talent. He earned a living by producing religious pictures for churches but also continued painting *bodegones.* Around this time Pacheco commissioned Velazquez to paint a portrait of a poet friend from Madrid. The two artists went to the capital city and visited the Escorial, the royal palace and church, which was filled with paintings from Italy and northern countries. The works of **Titian** (see entry) and other Venetian painters especially impressed Velazquez. Pacheco also brought his protégé to meet a friend who was part of the royal court. When Velazquez later painted a portrait of Pacheco's friend, the entire court, including King Philip IV, admired it greatly.

So impressed was the king, in fact, that the next year, 1623, he appointed Velazquez official court painter, an honor that included a salary, residence, and studio in the palace. Velazquez was in his early twenties. The king—himself a mere 18 years old—had a special chair placed in the studio so he could watch Velazquez paint, but he had to sit very still for the painter's first job: a portrait of His Majesty. The king was so pleased with the results that he insisted no one else would ever paint his portrait. Over the years Velazquez painted several portraits of Philip, leaving a visual chronicle of the king's maturation during his reign. Velazquez also depicted the king, queen, and prince on horseback and rendered the likenesses of other members of the court as well. He was a master at presenting these august figures as royal and impressive while detailing subtleties of character by adding unusual elements; his personal impressions of these subjects came through despite their stoically regal faces and costumes. Velazquez had little or no time for his *bodegones;* court painting absorbed all of his energies, though privately he may have found his privileged subjects less interesting than the street vendors and children of his family neighborhood.

Influenced by Rubens's court visit

When Velazquez had been at court for five years, an important visitor came from Antwerp on a diplomatic mission. **Peter Paul Rubens** (see entry), then the most famous painter in northern Europe, stayed with the royal family for nine months. The two painters spent a substantial amount of time together; Velazquez admired the older painter's skill, especially his brushwork and use of color. Rubens encouraged Velazquez to visit Italy to study the works of painting's great masters. In 1629— having obtained the king's permission—Velazquez traveled to Milan, Venice, and Rome, studying paintings by Titian, the Renaissance master **Michelangelo** (see entry), and sixteenth-century painter Tintoretto. He also sketched ancient Roman statues and paintings in the villas around Rome. These influences affected Velazquez's style, inspiring him to employ more brilliant colors and softer light.

When Velazquez returned to Madrid, the king appointed him to an additional position, *aposentador del rey,* usher to the king. He was now in charge of heating, lighting, and other environmental matters in the palace rooms, as well as all arrangements for the king when he traveled. This new occupation swallowed a great deal of Velazquez's painting time.

The Spanish court employed numerous dwarfs—people of unusually small stature whose bodily proportions are often abnormal—mostly as entertainers; Velazquez painted portraits of several of these court figures, either by themselves or with the princes and princesses, whom they often accompanied. In these portraits, Velazquez neither highlighted nor concealed the dwarfs' deformities, focusing instead on their faces to show them as intelligent, dignified people. This can be seen in his portraits *Don Antonio el Ingles* and *Don Diego de Acedo*.

Prefigures impressionism

In 1649 Velazquez was afforded another chance to expand his horizons; the king granted him permission to visit Italy again, and this time he stayed for more than two years, though King Philip continually urged him to return to Madrid. He visited Venice and Naples but devoted the majority of his time to Rome. He was welcomed there as one of Europe's premiere artists and was entertained by princes, cardinals, and the pope, head of the Catholic Church. He painted innumerable portraits during this portion of his travels. He also visited the villa of the Medici family, the great patrons of the **Renaissance,** where he completed sketches and paintings of garden settings. These scenes, full of dappled sunlight and color, are very similar to some of the open-air paintings done by the **impressionists** over two hundred years later.

Pope Innocent X asked Velazquez to paint his portrait; the result has been called the Spanish artist's masterpiece. The pope had coarse, ruddy features and a suspicious expression, but Velazquez did not flatter his revered subject. Rather, he painted him truthfully, even emphasizing the pontiff's coloring with the red satin of his clothing and the velvet throne on which he sat. The pope prized the honesty of Velazquez's work and was so pleased that he made the painter a member of the Roman Academy, a great honor.

Finally, King Philip insisted that Velazquez return to Madrid. The monarch had recently married a new, young queen, Mariana of Austria, who demanded festivities and entertainments. Responsibility for these arrangements fell to Velazquez; in addition, of course, he bore the burden of painting portraits of the queen, her company, and the children who were born in the next few years. The portrait of Mariana—painted about a year after she became queen, when she was 17 years old—depicts her in the voluminous, heavily decorated style of dress popular at the time. She also wears a large wig full of ribbons, feathers, and ornaments. The portrait does not convey much affection for Philip's bride on the part of the painter, as her face looks small and indistinct beneath the elaborate headdress.

Paints clever *Las Meninas*

One member of the royal family Velazquez did particularly enjoy was the little princess Margarita, who was born in 1651. He painted her portrait several times during the 1650s, and she is the central figure in his most famous painting, *Las Meninas (Maids of Honor)*. In this great work, Margarita stands in the center of the room, as though she has just burst into the painter's studio (shown with many of his paintings hanging on the walls), where he is engaged in painting a portrait of her mother and father. She pays no attention to the attendants on either side of her but seems instead to look at an area outside of the picture where the king and queen pose for the portrait; we know they are the object of Margarita's gaze because they appear in the mirror behind her. On the left we see Velazquez himself, standing in front of a huge canvas with his paintbrush in hand. This is the only known self-portrait of the painter. Two aspects of this work have delighted and intrigued generations of admirers: the lively cast of characters from the court—including a dog—and the reflections of the king and queen. *Las Meninas* challenges viewers to imagine the larger story behind the image. In terms of composition, it is a wonderful study of **perspective,** with clear and careful illustration of both the dog's paws in the very front of the space, to the man standing in the doorway deep in the back of the room. It is said that the king

made Velazquez a knight of the Order of Santiago, an extremely high honor, after seeing this painting.

Throughout the late 1650s, Velazquez became increasingly involved with his courtly duties. In the spring of 1660 he was required to plan the wedding of one of King Philip's daughters to the King of France. It was a huge affair on an island in the River Bidassoa, between Spain and France. Velazquez was charged with getting everything and everyone from Madrid to this island and arranging the food and festivities, all the while keeping the assembled royals and nobles happy and comfortable. The parade of animals, carriages, and wagons carrying people and supplies is said to have stretched for 18 miles. The burden of this huge project on the 61-year-old Velazquez was considerable; he fell ill and died a few weeks after the wedding.

Velazquez's influence has been tremendous. He left only about one hundred paintings, mostly portraits, but the quality of this relatively small body of work has been appreciated by many artists—later court painter **Francisco Goya,** early French impressionist **Edouard Manet,** Spanish cubist **Pablo Picasso,** Spanish surrealist **Salvador Dali** (see entries), Thomas Eakins, Fernando Botera, and Francis Bacon, to name but a few. He possessed a keen eye, a mastery of color and space, and great respect for his subjects, whether peasants or kings. Most of his paintings, national treasures, hang in the Prado Museum in Madrid.

Masterworks	
1618	*Old Woman Cooking Eggs*
1619	*Water Seller of Seville*
1624	*Philip IV*
1628	*Los Barrachos (The Drinkers)*
1634	*Prince Baltasar Carlos*
1644	*Don Diego de Acedo— El Primo*
1650	*View of Garden of Villa Medici— Noon and Evening*
	Juan de Pareja
	Pope Innocent X
1656	*Las Meninas (Maids of Honor)*
1657	*The Tapestry Weavers*

◀ Las Meninas (Maids of Honor), *1656. Oil on canvas, approx. 10'5" x 9'. Museo del Prado, Madrid. Reproduced by permission of Alinari/Art Resource, NY.*

Andy Warhol

Born August 6, c. 1928
Pittsburgh, Pennsylvania

Died February 22, 1987
New York, New York

"If you want to know all about Andy Warhol, just look at the surface of my paintings and films and me, and there I am. There's nothing behind it."

▲ *Portrait: Reproduced by permission of AP/Wide World Photos.*

Often called the father of **pop art**, Andy Warhol influenced a generation of artists with his irreverent approach to the fundamental question of what constitutes art. In so doing, he became a symbol of popular culture. As one writer said, "Even though most people are not sure exactly what Andy was famous *for*, his name permeates our culture ... it turns up everywhere." Warhol labored to maintain the image of the cool, jet-setting, pop artist, thronged wherever he went by a crowd of admirers. In fact, he excelled in a variety of media and fields, including commercial art, painting, film, publishing, and music. But he was an extremely quiet and private person who actually revealed very little about himself and his life.

Warhol was so mysterious about his private life, in fact, that his exact birth date is not generally known; most sources say 1928, but others give 1929 or 1930 as the year. His parents, Ondrej (Andrew, in Czech) and Julia Warhola, were emigrants from Czechoslovakia who settled in the Pittsburgh, Pennsylvania area. Warhol shortened the family name when he went to New York after college. He claimed to remember little of his childhood except that his father was often away on trips to the coal mines where he was employed. He also recalls his mother reading to him in her heavy Czech accent. She and Warhol were very close; she lived with him for many years in New York and often lent her hand to the curlicue lettering he used in his early commercial drawings.

Spent summer arranging window displays

Ondrej Warhola died when Warhol was 12. To help support his mother and two brothers, Warhol sold produce from the back of a truck. He also held a summer job at a local department store where he arranged window displays, scouring fashion magazines for inspiration. Warhol graduated from high school when he was 15 and somehow managed to amass enough money to enroll in the Carnegie Institute of Technology. He had decided to study art. He became part of a group of art students, many of whom already had successful careers. They lived together in an old barn and enjoyed a busy social life, throwing frequent parties and attending concerts. It was with these friends that Warhol first visited New York City and saw the works of modern artists like **Pablo Picasso** (see entry) at the Museum of Modern Art. Warhol did not do particularly well in college, but he did graduate in 1949.

After graduation Warhol moved with his friend and fellow artist Philip Pearlstein to New York City. He was very shy and rather shabbily turned out for the business and fashion worlds of New York, but some quality of his person and his work attracted people. He was hired immediately by *Glamour* magazine to produce illustrations for articles and advertisement drawings of women's shoes. Warhol's style was light and whimsical; he relied on black ink to define energetic outlines, with lots of flourishes and curls. He often used cupids, hearts, and tassels for their decorative effect and filled the drawings in with soft watercolors.

Warhol's career as a commercial artist bloomed throughout the 1950s. He worked very quickly and had a reputation for flexibility and a gift for satisfying his customers. He produced advertising and illustrations for numerous fashion magazines, shoe manufacturers, and department stores. He also contributed illustrations to book and album covers. Indeed, Warhol was so successful that he was able to buy a townhouse in Manhattan and hire assistants to complete his drawings. His work was exhibited in galleries, and he won several awards from advertising organizations.

Abandoned commercial art for "serious" painting

In 1960 Warhol's life changed abruptly; he abandoned commercial art and instead sought to become a "serious" painter. He knew the work of some of the "hot" new artists in New York, among them Jasper Johns and Robert Rauschenberg. They were challenging the **abstract expressionism** that had come to dominate the art scene in New York. It was a highly theoretical style in which the elements of composition—form, line, color—were employed to express emotion rather than to represent the physical world. Some felt the abstract expressionists took themselves too seriously; younger artists longed to reclaim art and bring it back to the world of the everyday. Warhol absorbed this notion and began painting images of ordinary subjects, including comic strips (Superman and Dick Tracy), Coca-Cola bottles, and Campbell's Soup cans. Warhol explained that he had soup every day for lunch and painted the cans just because they were there.

His new mode was not immediately applauded. He was turned down by one of New York's most prestigious galleries because it already represented an artist who painted comic strips—**Roy Lichtenstein** (see entry). Warhol finally got a break in 1962 when a gallery in Los Angeles showed his soup can paintings. These cans, Lichtenstein's comics, and the work of a few other artists gave birth to pop art. Critics and the public were divided over its merits. Some loved the new style, viewing it as commentary on the artificial nature of consumer society and a rebuttal to the somberness of the abstract expressionists; others thought it a bold-faced fraud.

Andy Warhol became the most famous of all the pop artists. He revealed an uncanny knack for making outrageous statements, attracting publicity, and choosing images that either shocked or exposed the falseness of social values. Around 1963 he began rendering his images in a commercial silk-screen printing process, producing them in a production line much like soup cans and other products are produced. This gave his images of dollar bills, Coke bottles, and movie stars a hard-edged, mass-produced look. It emphasized Warhol's notion that these subjects were as empty and meaningless as modern life itself.

Reflected consumer culture with soup cans, Coke bottles

Many of Warhol's works from these years are repetitive images. He painted *32 Soup Cans,* each one the same except for the name of the soup's flavor. He also unveiled *82 Two-Dollar Bills* and *210 Coke Bottles.* Multiple images of the Mona Lisa, the Statue of Liberty, and other important cultural symbols emerged as well. Some insisted that these works were simply not art. And still others regarded them as the perfect reflection of the mass-produced objects that were flooding American culture. Warhol reinforced this observation by calling his studio "The Factory." In the 1960s it became *the* hangout for pop culture groupies from around the country. Homeless teens, druggies, rock musicians, and other "subculture" types collected there. Warhol said that they stimulated his creativity.

The mid-1960s were an incredibly active time in the arts. Warhol produced his famous *Brillo Boxes,* three-dimensional replicas of the crates used to store and transport Brillo soap pads. Warhol had long loved the glamour and glitz of Hollywood, and he created many images of famous stars like Marilyn Monroe, Elvis Presley, Marlon Brando, and Elizabeth Taylor. Soon celebrities came flocking, asking him to silk-screen their portraits; it seemed that such attention from Warhol was a mark of success. Over the years, he produced dozens of canvases of people ranging from singers Mick Jagger and Liza Minnelli to heavyweight champ Muhammad Ali; in this manner he even captured

Campbell's Soup, *1968.*
© *1995 The Andy Warhol*
Foundation for Visual Arts.

the biggest 1960s cultural symbol of all, himself. He also produced a series of images of car accidents, bomb explosions, and other disasters. These repeated images of horrible events expressed Warhol's belief that people were becoming accustomed to such sights and were less and less affected by them. At the same time, he showed totally superficial works like *Cow Wall-paper* and bright, photograph-like images of flowers. To be sure, contradiction was part of his image.

In 1964 Warhol began experimenting with a new media, making several underground films during the next few years. Many were long and deliberately tedious. Warhol said his aim was to take an art form defined by movement and show as little movement as possible. *Haircut,* for instance, is a 45-minute film of a Factory hanger-on getting a haircut. Most of these films have one-word titles like *Sleep, Kiss, Eat,* and *Face.* Some of Warhol's films and other projects of the late 1960s became laden with bizarre and violent imagery. Music, too, was part of the mix; Warhol sponsored a fledgling rock band called the Velvet Underground that would go on to international fame. He explained his forays outside the canvas by saying, "The Pop idea was that anybody could do anything, so naturally we were all trying to do it all."

The pop artist becomes pop star

Warhol himself was becoming such a pop star that crowds gathered wherever he appeared. He maintained an image of a silent, ultracool, almost android-like tastemaker. He was known for his silver-dyed hair; later he colored his hair black and wore a spiky blond wig on top of it. At an opening in Philadelphia, his paintings had to be taken down because museum officials feared they would be damaged by mobs of unruly fans. In typical style, Warhol commented, "It was fabulous. An art opening with no art!" The scene came crashing to a halt, however, in June 1968 when one of Warhol's Factory crowd shot and nearly killed him. It took him almost a year to recover.

Warhol and his Factory were greatly changed after that. The actual Factory was painted white, made incredibly clean and antiseptic, and had a security system installed; it became a more elegant salon for the rich and famous who came to be "done" by Warhol. Around this time Warhol took on magazine publishing. *Interview* magazine became a hot item for gossip about the jet set, news of the latest fashions, and interviews with

"the beautiful people." *Interview* is especially remembered for its famous motto, which stated that in the future, everyone would be famous for 15 minutes.

The 1970s were a more subdued but still glamorous time for Warhol. One writer commented that when Warhol "wasn't at the White House or [fashion designer] Halston's apartment, he was often at the decade's leading disco, Studio 54." Warhol continued his portraiture, and many of his other works were commissions from wealthy clients. He also produced works that many felt bordered on pornography; nonetheless, his creations were exhibited in museums and galleries around the world. In the 1980s Warhol embraced social and political causes, offering his labor to the Save the Children campaign and the Jimmy Carter Presidential Library. He also undertook a series of drawings of endangered animals that was shown at the American Museum of Natural History in New York. Moreover, the 1980s found Warhol boosting the careers of young artists whose work has also made a mark on "postmodern" art, including Keith Haring and Jean-Michel Basquiat.

Masterworks

1961	*32 Soup Cans*
1962	*The Two Marilyns*
1963	*Orange Car Crash*
1964	*Flowers*
	Triple Elvis
	Brillo Box
1966	*Cow Wallpaper*
1967	*Double Self-Portrait*
1975	*Mick Jagger*
1978	*Liza Minnelli*
1983	*Endangered Species: Bald Eagle*

Warhol's death following surgery in 1987 shocked the art world. But as would be expected, he continued to arouse controversy even after his demise. The impenetrable image of the passive artist who thrived on the speed and superficiality of modern life was shattered when it was revealed that Warhol was a devout Catholic who spent many volunteer hours working in soup kitchens; the Factory was a "front" for his private townhouse, which was filled with beautiful furniture, traditional art, and large collections of "disposable art," including one of fanciful cookie jars. It took auctioneers ten days to sell Warhol's belongings, the auction itself becoming a cultural event.

Warhol's work remains a source of delight and debate. Several museums have hung large exhibitions since his death. In 1994 the Andy Warhol Museum was opened in his hometown of Pittsburgh. It is the largest museum in the United States devoted to a single artist, with more than 500 of his works on display. On the first day of its opening, the museum attracted more than 14,000 visitors. Among them were the beautiful people who still wanted to be associated with Warhol, including politicians, artists, and movie stars. Warhol would surely have loved that even after his death, he and his art held the spotlight. Argument continues as to whether the spotlight illuminates an important, enduring body of work, or whether Warhol was simply an expert "put-on" artist. Either way, as one observer said, "He was out front ... in pinning down how it was to live in the 60s, 70s, and 80s."

Frank Lloyd Wright

Born June 8, 1867
Richland Center, Wisconsin

Died April 9, 1959
Phoenix, Arizona

The name Frank Lloyd Wright has become virtually synonymous with architecture in the American mind. Wright was a flamboyant, outspoken figure who was both praised and criticized for his controversial ideas about space and design. His restlessness and unbridled creativity gave rise to what he called his "organic" style. He was a master of technological concepts that would not become prominent until well after his heyday, and his productivity was legendary—Wright designed thousands of buildings, almost 800 of which were constructed. Each of his projects was unique. The body of work they represent continues to influence architects almost 40 years after Wright's death.

Wright's mother was sure her son would be an architect. Anna Lloyd-Jones Wright was a strong-willed, intelligent, and shy woman who taught school for many years. She claimed that before her son was born, she decorated the nursery with pictures of cathedrals from England so he would grow up to build beautiful buildings.

"What I am seeking is a genuine living architecture of the present."

▲ *Portrait: Reproduced by permission of UPI/Bettmann.*

Anna Wright was the second wife of William Cary Wright, a minister. William Wright had three children from his first marriage, and he and Anna had three more. This large family moved often as William Wright served as minister for a variety of congregations in Wisconsin and Massachusetts. When Frank Lloyd Wright was about 12, they settled in Madison, Wisconsin. Some of his mother's relatives lived on a farm in the nearby town of Spring Green. As a teenager, Wright spent several summers working on his uncle's farm. He came to love the countryside of the area and eventually built a house there.

Became draftsman to help support family

As a boy Wright loved to read and "invent" things. But he did not enjoy school, disdaining the many rules he encountered there and deeming most of the curriculum useless; he quit high school just before graduation. At the time, his parents were in the midst of a divorce. Ultimately, Wright's father left, and the two never saw each other again. To help support the family, Wright took a job as a draftsman in the office of the city's civil engineer, making exact scale drawings of city buildings, roads, sewers, and the like. Wright displayed great talent for this work. Soon he began to share his mother's dream of him becoming an architect.

Wright's boss was also the dean of the engineering school at the University of Wisconsin in Madison. He was able to bend the rules and allow Wright to enroll without a high school diploma. There were few architecture schools in the United States in the 1880s; most would-be architects studied engineering, rarely developing new styles of design and mostly copying traditional structures while changing details and adding decoration. Popular designs included the neoclassicism of Greek temples, as well as the conventions of Egyptian and French architecture. Wright remained in engineering school for roughly 18 months before frustration with these creative constraints drove him to leave at the age of 20.

Despite his mother's objections, Wright left Madison and arrived in Chicago in 1887 with seven dollars in his pocket. With an uncle's help he landed a job in an architect's office where he helped design houses. These residences adhered to the traditional style of the period, characterized by large porches, turrets, and overhanging roofs. Wright soon became unsatisfied with this work. Eventually he won a position at the most important architecture firm in Chicago, Adler & Sullivan. The heads of this firm, Dankmar Adler and Louis Sullivan, had built several of the most important and progressively designed buildings in Chicago.

Followed function with form

Wright was intrigued by Sullivan's conviction that "form follows function," that the design of a structure should be determined by the structure's purpose. This became a key element of Wright's philosophy of architecture. He rose quickly in the firm, becoming chief draftsman and working his way toward an impressive salary within a year. He married Catherine Tobin in 1889 and settled in Oak Park, a prosperous town near Chicago. His mother and two sisters joined him and lived in a house next door. Wright and his wife had six children.

In 1894 Wright opened his own architecture firm and became busy designing homes for his prosperous Oak Park neighbors. By 1900 he had developed a new mode, the Prairie Style, based on the idea that a residence should blend into its surroundings. Wright believed that in the flat and wide midwestern landscape, houses should be similarly flat and wide. Prairie-style houses were comprised of one or two stories, with broad roofs and long rows of windows emphasizing their horizontal orientation. Wright also remade the interior space of the house; while traditional residences were divided into box-like rooms, Wright was convinced that the space should be more free-flowing and echo in design the exterior of the structure. The primary space of the house was frequently centered around a stone fireplace. This unity of environment was called the organic style. Wright even designed the furniture, rugs, tableware, and more to maintain consistency. The Robie House and the Willits House, both in the Chicago area, are fully realized examples of Wright's Prairie Style.

During the early 1900s Wright also designed two innovative public buildings. The Larkin Building in Buffalo, New

York, was the first office building in the country to feature metal furniture, plate-glass windows, and air conditioning. Wright also included a recreation area and restaurant on the premises. His Unity Temple church in Oak Park was a pioneering structure because it was the first public building to be made of poured concrete.

By 1910 Wright's reputation was spreading. A book illustrating his work was published in Germany and began to influence European architects. He visited there to great acclaim that year. The trip was tainted by scandal, however, because Wright had left his wife and children behind and traveled with a married woman, Mamah Borthwick Cheney. When they returned from Europe, Wright built a new house for himself and Cheney near his old home of Spring Green, Wisconsin. He called the residence Taliesin, Welsh for "shining brow." It was a secluded retreat, constructed of materials from the area, that boasted a farm and studio.

Wright and Cheney lived there only about three years before tragedy struck: a mentally unstable household worker went on a murderous rampage, killing Cheney, her two children, and four others and burning the house to the ground. Wright was devastated. But rather than abandon the site, he rebuilt the house, naming it Taliesin II and dedicating it to Cheney.

Vindicated by Tokyo earthquake

From 1915 to 1922 Wright was consumed by the design and construction of the Imperial Hotel in Tokyo, Japan. This project was challenging in that its setting is prone to earthquakes. Wright's solution to this potential problem was criticized by many. The hotel was built on a deep bed of mud, with the foundation sunk only a short way into the ground. Wright reasoned that the hotel would be able to "sway" in the event of a quake, but would not "break" from stress. His theory was tested just a year after the hotel was finished when a major trembler struck Tokyo. Almost 100,000 people were killed in collapsing buildings and fires; the Imperial Hotel was the only large building left standing.

This vindication served to increase Wright's already strong sense of self-assurance and independence. In fact, he was renowned as difficult—inflexible, opinionated, and stubborn. These qualities were apparently only matched by his sense of superiority. He once asserted, "Not only do I intend to be the greatest architect who has ever lived, but the greatest who will ever live." His radical design principles and rampant egotism combined to create an eccentric persona. Wright was certain that his way was the way of the future, and by and large, he was right.

The 1920s represented a low point in Wright's career. He met and married sculptor Miriam Noel (his first wife divorced him in 1922), but they were divorced within a short time. Taliesin II burned in 1925, and Wright exhausted his fortune rebuilding it. He was often short on funds but could not seem to stop spending. When the bank threatened to foreclose on Taliesin III, a group of Wright's friends and relatives came to his aid. During this period he received few commissions, focusing instead on lecturing and writing.

Fallingwater, the Kaufmann House, in Bear Run, Pennsylvania, 1936-39. Reproduced by permission of The Bettmann Archive.

471 | Frank Lloyd Wright

In 1928 Wright married his third wife, Olgivanna Hinzenberg. Their relationship lasted 30 years, until Wright's death. Olgivanna provided him with much support and stability over the course of some of his most creative years. She was also responsible for maintaining the Taliesin Fellowship Wright had established long after the architect's death. Wright began the fellowship as an apprentice and teaching program at Taliesin III in the 1930s. Student apprentices assisted Wright with his commissions, benefiting immeasurably from the hands-on training, and contributed to the Taliesin community by working in the gardens, farm, kitchen, or wherever they were needed. In 1938 Wright built a "winter home" for the Fellowship called Taliesin West near Phoenix, Arizona. Many of the fellows became close to Wright and considered themselves disciples of a great master.

Fallingwater

Wright's other major achievement of the 1930s was an amazing residence in the hills of Pennsylvania. He was commissioned by Pittsburgh businessman Edgar Kaufmann to build a country house for his family. The wooded property he owned was graced by a waterfall, and this is where Wright chose to build the house—over the waterfall. The stunning result, called Fallingwater, meshes perfectly with its setting. It displays all of Wright's concepts of organic design, among them the use of materials native to the area; interior and exterior spaces flowing into each other; and a central fireplace as the focus of the household. One historian called it "the most famous modern house in the world." Now open to the public, people flock from all over the world to visit Fallingwater and marvel at its beauty.

In 1936 Wright began work on the acclaimed headquarters of the Johnson Wax Company in Racine, Wisconsin. Particularly noteworthy are the structure's support columns, described alternately as tall, thin mushrooms or giant golf tees topped by massive discs. Wright also designed 18 buildings for the campus of Florida State College during this period. Moreover, he developed a plan for construction of inexpensive, middle-class housing that was remarkable for its many work-saving innova-

tions. Some of these "Usonian" homes—named for the first letters in United States—were built throughout the country in the late 1930s and early 1940s. Wright also designed many homes for wealthy patrons in these years, as well as during the 1950s.

Wright's final, most famous, and arguably most controversial project was the Solomon R. Guggenheim Museum in New York City. Nothing like it had ever been built. It was made of concrete and took the form of a gigantic spiral ramp; there are no rooms, just continuous gallery space. New Yorkers claimed it resembled a giant snail or spiral cinnamon bun. Needless to say, the Guggenheim contrasted markedly with the traditional buildings surrounding it. Artists feared that their works would not hang properly on the upward-sloping walls. In typical fashion, Wright proved everyone wrong. Though he died a few months before the museum was completed and was thus deprived the last laugh, today the Guggenheim is universally recognized as one of the world's great landmarks.

Solomon R. Guggenheim Museum, New York City, 1957-59. Reinforced concrete; diameter at ground level 100', height of dome 92'. Reproduced by permission of Photos/Camera Press.

Masterworks

1902	Willits House, Highland Park, Illinois
1904	Larkin Company Administration Building, Buffalo, New York
1906	Unity Temple, Oak Park, Illinois
1909	Robie House, Chicago, Illinois
1911, 1914, 1925	Taliesin, Spring Green, Wisconsin
1922	Imperial Hotel, Tokyo, Japan
1936-39	Fallingwater (Kaufmann House), Bear Run, Pennsylvania
1936-46	S. C. Johnson and Son Co. (Johnson Wax) Administration Building, Racine, Wisconsin
1938	Taliesin West, near Phoenix, Arizona
1954	Beth Shalom Synagogue, Elkins Park, Pennsylvania
1957-59	Solomon R. Guggenheim Museum, New York, New York

Wright is remembered as a genius whose uniquely "modern" ideas were far ahead of their time. He worked until he was 92 years old with vitality and conviction. Though his irritable nature may not have made him the most-loved architect in history, he is certainly among the greatest, as the numerous laurels bestowed upon him attest. One of the plans he left behind at his death was for a mile-high skyscraper. As one writer put it, "The sky was the only limit for Frank Lloyd Wright."

Further Reading

Christo

Arenas, Jose F., *The Key to Renaissance Art,* Lerner, 1990.

Bracons, Jose, *The Key to Gothic Art,* Lerner, 1990.

Chase, Alice Elizabeth, *Famous Artists of the Past,* Platt & Munk, 1964.

Cirlot, Lourdes, *The Key to Modern Art of the Early Twentieth Century,* Lerner, 1990.

Cook, J., *Understanding Modern Art,* E D C Publishing, 1992.

Frayling, Christopher, Helen Frayling, and Ron van der Meer, *The Art Pack,* Knopf, 1992.

Greenberg, Jan, and Sandra Jordan, *The Painter's Eye: Learning to Look at Contemporary American Art,* Delacorte, 1991.

Greenberg, Jan, and Sandra Jordan, *The Sculptor's Eye: Looking at Contemporary American Art,* Delacorte, 1993.

Isaacson, Philip M., *A Short Walk around the Pyramids and through the World of Art,* Knopf, 1993.

Janson, H. W., and Anthony E. Janson, *History of Art for Young People,* 4th ed., Abrams, 1982.

Kennet, Frances, *Looking at Painting,* Marshall Cavendish, 1990.

Reyero, Carlos, *The Key to Art from Romanticism to Impressionism,* Lerner, 1990.

Salvi, Francesco, *The Impressionists: The Origin of Modern Painting,* Peter Bedrick Books, 1994.

Triado, Juan-Ramon, *The Key to Baroque Art,* Lerner, 1990.

Ventura, Piero, *Great Painters,* Putnam, 1984.

Woolf, Felicity, *Picture This Century: An Introduction to Twentieth-Century Art,* Doubleday, 1992.

Index

*Bolds indicate biographees
and volume numbers;
illustrations are marked by (ill.).*

Yellow Calla
by Georgia O'Keeffe

Clair, René **2:** 284

Claude Monet in His Floating Studio (Manet) **2:** 278

Cliff at Etretat (Monet) **2:** 314

Cock, Hieronymous **1:** 30

Collage **1:** 19-20, 98

Cologne, Germany **1:** 83

Colonia Güell (Barcelona) **1:** 133

Composition I (Improvisation) (Kandinsky) **1:** 206

Concerning the Spiritual in Art **1:** 207

Constantinople **1:** 160

Correggio **1:** 50-51

Couture, Thomas **2:** 273-274

Cow's Skull: Red, White, and Blue (O'Keeffe) **2:** 334

The Creation (Michelangelo) **2:** 302 (ill.)

Cubism **1:** 104-105, 110-111; **2:** 306-307, 344-349

Cybernetics **1:** 39

D

Dadaism **1:** 110-111; **2:** 281-282, 286-287

Daguerre, Louis **2:** 274

Dali, Salvador 1: 89-95

David (Michelangelo) **2:** 300

Da Vinci, Leonardo (*see* **Leonardo da Vinci**)

Davis, Edward Wyatt **1:** 96

Davis, Stuart 1: 96-102, 111, 210

Day, Benjamin **2:** 259

Dead Souls **1:** 70

The Dead Toreador (Manet) **2:** 275

"Death" (Kollwitz) **1:** 215-216

Death Seizing a Woman (Kollwitz) **1:** 215 (ill.)

Decorative Arts Museum **2:** 392

Degas, Edgar **1:** 48, 50-51, 53, 148; **2:** 277, 278, 314, 366

de Kooning, Elaine **1:** 123-124

de Kooning, Willem **1:** 123-124, 210

Delacroix, Eugene **1:** 152

Derain, Andre **2:** 294

De Stijl **2:** 307

Detroit Industry (Rivera) **2:** 383

Detroit Institute of Arts **1:** 22; **2:** 383

Deutscher Werkbund **1:** 167

Diaghilev, Serge **2:** 348

Diego and I (Kahlo) **1:** 200 (ill.)

Dinner at Aunt Connie's House **2:** 377

The Dinner Party (Chicago) **1:** 78-81, 79 (ill.)

Diploma (Hockney) **1:** 184

Dividing Line (Kandinsky) **1:** 209

Don Antonio el Ingles (Velazquez) **2:** 454

Donatello **1:** 70; **2:** 294, 297

Doncieux, Camille **2:** 311-313

Don Diego de Acedo (Velazquez) **2:** 454

Dos de Mayo (*The Second of May;* Goya) **1:** 155-156

Douglass College **2:** 259

Douglass, Frederick **2:** 239

Dove, Arthur **2:** 421

Duchamp, Marcel 1: 38-39, **103-112,** 201-202, 209; **2:** 281, 287

Duchamp, Suzanne **1:** 103-104

Duchamp-Villon, Raymond **1:** 103

Dürer, Albrecht 1: 113-121, 148

E

Eakins, Thomas **2:** 425

Easter and the Totem (Pollock) **2:** 355-356

"Eggbeater Series" (Davis) **1:** 98

The Eiffel Tower (Seurat) **2:** 415

El Espolio (*The Disrobing of Christ;* El Greco) **1:** 162

El Greco (*see* **Greco, El**)

Eluard, Gala **1:** 94

The Endless Column (Brancusi) **1:** 27

The Enemy Would Have Been Warned ... That My Ship Was Below Them (Lichtenstein) **2:** 261 (ill.)

Engravings **1:** 113, 115-116

Environmental art **1:** 82-88

"Equivalents" series (Stieglitz) **2:** 422

Goya, Francisco **1:** 70, 119,
  152-157; **2:** 368
Graham, Martha **2:** 327
Great Berlin Art Exhibit (1898)
  1: 213
Great Depression **1:** 98-100
The Great Migration (Lawrence)
  2: 239
El Greco **1:** 119, **158-165**; **2:** 436
Greenberg, Clement **1:** 123-125
The Green Box (Duchamp) **1:** 109
The Green Sound (Kandinsky)
  1: 209
The Green Violinist (Chagall) **1:** 71
Gris, Juan **2:** 343, 345-346
Groovin' High (Ringgold) **2:** 375
Gropius House (Lincoln, Massachu-
  setts; Gropius) **1:** 170 (ill.)
Gropius, Walter 1: 166-173, 209;
  2: 338
Grosz, George **1:** 16
Groundswell (Lin) **2:** 270
Grygo, George **1:** 175
Güell, Finca **1:** 132
Güell i Bacigalupi, Eusebi
  1: 130-133
Güell Park (Barcelona) **1:** 133-134
Guernica (Picasso) **2:** 348 (ill.)
Guernica, Spain **2:** 348
Guggenheim, Peggy **2:** 353
Guggenheim, Solomon **1:** 210
Guillebon, Jeanne-Claude **1:** 83

H

Haircut (Warhol) **2:** 463
Haiti **2:** 238
Hanson, Duane 1: 174-180
Hard Hat (Hanson) **1:** 179
Haring, Keith **2:** 465
Harlem Community Art Center
  2: 408
Harlem Cultural Council **1:** 20
Harlem, New York **2:** 236-238
Harlem Renaissance **2:** 236, 406
Harlem Renaissance Party
  (Ringgold) **2:** 376
Harmony in Red (Matisse) **2:** 291
  (ill.), 292

Harper's Bazaar **1:** 97
Harriet and the Promised Land
  (Lawrence) **2:** 242
Hartigan, Grace **1:** 124
Hartley, Marsden **2:** 421
Hartzell, Joseph **2:** 425
Harvard Graduate Center **1:** 172
Harvard Graduate School of Design
  1: 171-172
Harvard University **2:** 267
Havemeyer, Louisine Elder **1:** 55
Haystack (Monet) **2:** 316 (ill.)
Hemmings, Emmy **2:** 286
Henri, Robert **1:** 97, 191
Henry Ford Hospital (Kahlo) **1:** 201
Hines, Earl "Fatha" **1:** 100
History of Mexico (Rivera)
  2: 381-382
Hitler, Adolf **1:** 71
Hobitza, Gorj, Romania **1:** 23
Hochedé, Alice **2:** 313, 316
Hochedé, Ernest **2:** 313, 316
Hockney, David 1: 181-189
Hoffman, Hans **1:** 210
Holbein, Hans **1:** 50
Holocaust **1:** 80-81
The Holocaust Project (Chicago)
  1: 80
Holty, Carl **1:** 17
Homer **1:** 17
Hopper, Edward 1: 190-196
Horace E. Dodge Fountain (Detroit;
  Noguchi) **2:** 328 (ill.)
Hotel Room (Hopper) **1:** 194
House by the Railroad (Hopper)
  1: 194
House of Squam Light (Hopper)
  1: 193
Hunters in the Snow (Bruegel)
  1: 32-33 (ill.)

I

I and the Village (Chagall) **1:** 66
  (ill.), 68
Imperial Hotel (Tokyo, Japan)
  2: 470
Impression: Sunrise (Monet)
  2: 312-314, 312 (ill.), 366

New York, New York **1:** 2, 4-6
New York World's Fair (1939)
  2: 327, 408
Nighthawks (Hopper) **1:** 195-196,
  195 (ill.)
Nightview, New York, 1932 (Abbott)
  1: 5 (ill.)
The Night Watch (Rembrandt)
  2: 361, 362 (ill.)
Nivinson, Josephine "Jo"
  1: 193-194
Noguchi, Isamu 1: 28; **2: 324-329**
Noguchi, Yone **2:** 324
Noland, Kenneth **1:** 125
Nude Descending a Staircase, No. 2
  (Duchamp) **1:** 105, 106 (ill.), 111
Number 23, 1948 (Pollock) **2:** 353
  (ill.)
Nuremberg, Germany **1:** 120-121

O

Ocean Greyness (Pollock)
  2: 355-356
Ohio State University **2:** 270
O'Keeffe, Georgia 1: 12;
  2: 330-335, 421
Oldenburg, Claes **2:** 262
Old Woman Cooking Eggs
  (Velazquez) **2:** 452
Olympia (Manet) **2:** 277, 279
Olympic Games (1992) **1:** 136
Op art **1:** 39
Organic Style **2:** 469
Orozco, José Clemente **2:** 382
Orpheus **2:** 329
Outbreak (Kollwitz) **1:** 213 (ill.)

P

Pacheco, Francisco **1:** 120;
  2: 451-452
Pacific Stock Exchange (San
  Francisco) **2:** 383
The Painter's Family (Matisse)
  2: 292
Palacio Nacional (Mexico City)
  2: 381
Palau Güell (Barcelona) **1:** 132-133

Parau Parau (*Conversations ou Les
  Pontins;* Gauguin) **1:** 140 (ill.)
Parayre, Amelie **2:** 290
Paris, France **1:** 4, 24, 48-51, 68;
  2: 290, 437-443
Paris Salon exhibition (1866) **1:** 50
Paris Salon exhibition (1868) **1:** 50
Paris Salon exhibition (1870) **1:** 50
Paris Salon exhibition (1872) **1:** 51
Paris Salon exhibition (1874) **1:** 51
*Pearblossom Hwy. 11-18th April
  1986* (Hockney) **1:** 186-187
The Peasant Dance (Bruegel) **1:** 32
"Peasants' War" (Kollwitz) **1:** 214
The Peasant Wedding (Bruegel)
  1: 31-32, 31 (ill.)
Pei, I. M. 2: 336-341
Pennsylvania Station (New York)
  2: 270
Pepper Jelly Lady (Bearden) **1:** 18
  (ill.)
The Persistence of Memory
  (*Persistence de la mémoire;* Dali)
  1: 90 (ill.), 91-92
The Pesaro Madonna (Titian)
  2: 432 (ill.)
Phalanx **1:** 205
Pharmacy (Duchamp) **1:** 107
Philip II (of Spain) **1:** 161-162;
  2: 433-435, 452-457
Photocollage **1:** 186
*Photographs: Annie Leibovitz 1970-
  1990* **2:** 248
Photojournalism **1:** 42-47
Photomontage **1:** 19-21
Photo-Secessionists **2:** 421
Picabia, Francis **1:** 110-111;
  2: 281, 287
Picasso Museum **2:** 349
Picasso, Pablo 1: 17, 24, 68, 90,
  97, 104, 110, 132, 141, 183, 202,
  210; **2:** 281, **342-349,** 352, 380,
  395, 421
Pietà (Michelangelo) **2:** 298-300,
  299 (ill.)
Pietà (Titian) **2:** 436
Pirckheimer, Willibald **1:** 114-115
Pissarro, Camille **1:** 50, 59-60, 138,
  148; **2:** 277, 312-314, 366, 412

The Umbrellas, Joint Project for Japan and USA (Christo) **1:** 86-87

Un Chien Andalou **1:** 94

Underground Railroad **2:** 239

UNESCO building (Paris) **2:** 323, 327

Unity Temple church (Oak Park, Illinois; Wright) **2:** 470

University of Mexico's National Preparatory School **2:** 381

University of the District of Columbia **1:** 80

University of Washington **2:** 242

U.S. Coast Guard **2:** 240-241

U.S. Embassy (Athens, Greece) **1:** 172

"Usonian" homes **2:** 473

U. S. Postage Stamp Commemorating the Advent of Black Power (Ringgold) **2:** 372-374

V

Van Aelst, Pieter Coecke **1:** 30

Van der Rohe, Mies **1:** 171

Van Doesburg, Theo **2:** 307

Van Dyck, Anthony **2:** 400, 435

Van Gogh, Vincent (*see* **Gogh, Vincent van**)

Vanity Fair **2:** 247

Van Rijn, Rembrandt (*see* **Rembrandt van Rijn**)

Vasarely, Victor **1:** 39

Vecelli, Tiziano (*see* **Titian**)

Velazquez, Diego 1: 50, 70, 152-153, 162; **2:** 274, 368, 402, **451-457**

Velvet Underground **2:** 463

Vence, France **2:** 293

Venice, Italy **1:** 158-160

Venus and Adonis (Titian) **2:** 435

Venus of Urbino (Titian) **2:** 435

Vermeer, Jan **1:** 92

Veronese **1:** 30; **2:** 436

Verrocchio, Andrea del **2:** 251

Vietnam Veterans Memorial (Washington, D.C.; Lin) **2:** 265-269 (ill.), 267 (ill.)

Vietnam war **1:** 177

View of Toledo (El Greco) **1:** 164 (ill.), 165

Villon, Jacques **1:** 103

Vinci, Leonardo da (*see* **Leonardo da Vinci**)

Violon d'Ingres (Man Ray) **2:** 285-286, 285 (ill.)

The Virgin of the Rocks (Leonardo) **2:** 253

"The Virtues" (Bruegel) **1:** 30

The Vision after the Sermon (Jacob Wrestling the Angel) (Gauguin) **1:** 141

A Visit with Christopher and Dean (Hockney) **1:** 188

Vlaminck, Maurice de **2:** 294

Votive paintings **1:** 201

W

The Wake and Resurrection of the Bicentennial Negro (Ringgold) **2:** 375

Wallace, Robert Earl **2:** 372

War (Hanson) **1:** 177

Warhol, Andy 2: 259, 262-263, **458-466**

"War" (Kollwitz) **1:** 214

The Water Seller (Velazquez) **2:** 452

"A Weaver's Rebellion" (Kollwitz) **1:** 212

The Wedding Dance (Bruegel) **1:** 32

We Greet Three, Mary (Ia Orana Maria; Gauguin) **1:** 142

Wenner, Jann **2:** 244

What the Water Gave Me (Kahlo) **1:** 201

Where Do We Come From? What Are We? Where Are We Going? (Gauguin) **1:** 142-143

Whitman, Walt **1:** 183

Whitney Museum of American Art **1:** 177

Who's Bad? (Ringgold) **2:** 375-376

Willits House (Wright) **2:** 469

Winter—Fifth Avenue (Stieglitz) **2:** 419-421